MYTH
AND
MONSTERS

BRIAN
HAWKINS

MYTHS & MONSTERS

CARIAD

© Copyright Brian Hawkins 1993

All rights reserved. No part of this publication may be reproduced. This book is sold subject to the condition that it shall not, by way of trade or otherwise, be lost, re-sold, hired out or otherwise circulated without the publisher's prior consent in any form of binding or cover other than that in which it is published, and without similar condition, including this condition being imposed on the subsequent purchaser.

Published in 1994 by CARIAD BOOKS, 28 Oaten Hill, Canterbury, Kent, England CT1 3HZ

A CIP catalogue record for this book is available from the British Library.

Printed for CARIAD
by INTYPE, Woodman Works, Durnsford Road, Wimbledon SW19 8DR

Cover "Theseus slaying the Minotaur" taken from an ancient Greek Vase by permission of the British Museum ©.
Layout design by Patricia Adkins, Brian Hawkins and John Barton.

ISBN 0-9516241-3-X

A MESSAGE TO YOUNGER READERS:

This book is primarily meant for you, who it is hoped will find the Greek Myths fascinating stories which are hundreds of years old. As you read these stories you will be able to use your imagination to build up a picture in your mind of what these men and monsters looked like.

Some of these stories can still be seen depicted in art galleries throughout the world. You will also come across references to them in poetry and literature. Therefore, a knowledge of Greek Mythology will help you to understand and appreciate the finest of these works.

Have fun and enjoy these classic tales.

For Holly and Katie who enjoyed my stories also Sebastian, Adam, Marcus and Eleanor, and with thanks to my wife, Jane, for all her patience and hard work on the word processor.

CONTENTS

Title	Page
Birth of the Gods	1
Hephaestus (Roman Vulcan)	5
Athene	7
Artemis and Apollo	9
Hermes, a Greek God	12
Dionysus	16
Prometheus	19
Melampus	23
Perseus	27
Bellerophon	36
Introduction to the Story of Jason & The Golden Fleece	41
Jason and the Golden Fleece	42
Theseus	57
Minos and the Minotaur	63
End of Minos	69
Theseus Visits the Underworld	72
How the Trojan War Started	76
Orpheus and Eurydice (A tale of Love and Tragedy)	84
Heracles	92
The Twelve Labours of Heracles	100
Further Adventures of Heracles	116

THE BIRTH OF THE GODS

There is a theory that our world started when a large portion of the sun dislodged itself and shot into outer space. As it cooled down and vaporised water appeared, then from that, plant life gradually came into being followed by insects and animal life. These grew and grew over the years until eventually we had the pre-historic monsters.

The Greeks called the earth Ge, and Ge is still used in English meaning the earth in such words as geography, geology, geocentric, geophysics etc. They considered the earth or Ge a goddess and knew her as "Mother Earth", the mother of all things. The rain they thought was a god called Uranus. Now Uranus and Ge (rain and earth) gave birth to various monsters. For instance, there were some the Greeks called the hundred handed ones, who may have been the ancestors of the octopus. Some giants they produced were called Titans, who were considered more intelligent than other monsters. Finally Ge gave birth to Cronus who was the ancestor of man, and then Rhea who was the ancestor of woman.

Cronus was not really very nice, because when he grew up he was jealous of his father and decided to get rid of him. To do this he waited until his father Uranus was asleep, took a sharp scythe and cut off some parts of his father's anatomy and threw them into the sea. These parts and the sea combined together and produced Aphrodite (the Roman Venus) who rose from the ocean and became the goddess of love, and so love was brought into the world.

Cronus having deposed his father, Uranus, married Rhea and they brought several children into the world. This rather worried Cronus as he thought that perhaps one of them would do the same to him as he had done to his father, therefore, every time Rhea gave birth he simply swallowed the child. The first was Hestia, then Demeter followed by Hera, all of whom were girls, the next two were boys, Poseidon and Hades. As you can imagine Rhea was getting very fed up with this situation, as any mother would, so she decided that the next child she had she would somehow manage to keep. Now it so happened that in the dead of night she gave birth to Zeus and immediately gave him to Mother Earth who hurriedly took him away to Crete and hid him in the cave of Dicte. (This cave is still in Crete and you can see where Zeus was hidden and secretly brought up if you ever go there). Rhea wrapped a stone in swaddling clothes and gave it to Cronus who, thinking it was his baby, swallowed it.

Zeus grew up in hiding and when fully grown worked out a plan to get revenge on his father. First he got a job as cup bearer to his father, of course Cronus did not know who he was as he had no idea that Zeus was alive, he thought that he had swallowed him. One day when Zeus took Cronus his usual drink of liquid honey, he added to it a mixture of some nasty tasting ingredients. I am not sure what they were, but I think something like bitter herbs, sea salt, castor oil, senna pods etc. Cronus was a greedy individual and swallowed all this in one gulp. Naturally, it made him sick and the first thing he brought up was the stone which, of course, was the last thing he had swallowed. This stone landed at Delphi and it is still there as you will see for yourself if you ever go to Delphi. Next Cronus brought up the children he had swallowed, who then were fully grown up. They overpowered their father and banished him to some terrible place on the other side of the world. Naturally they were all pleased with their sudden freedom and as Zeus was responsible for this they elected him their leader.

It was then decided between them which duties each should perform. This resulted in Zeus being the god of the sky and heavens; Poseidon, the god of the sea and Hades the god of the underworld. Hestia became the goddess of the hearth, important not only for cooking, but also for warmth of the fire needed in winter. Demeter was to be the goddess of corn, vegetation and the fruits and riches of the field.

Hera married Zeus and became Queen of the sky and, as she was now the wife of the most powerful god, she was represented as the ideal wife and became the goddess of marriage and maternity. This marriage was the only true marriage among the Olympian Gods. Zeus and Hera had four children. The first was a charming girl named Hebe. She was so helpful and ever willing to run errands for the gods. Whenever Zeus or Hera felt thirsty

Hebe always seemed to be at hand with a cup of nectar (the wine of the gods) ready for them to quench their thirst. Hera next gave birth to twins, a boy and a girl, who were certainly not nearly as nice as their sister.

The boy was Ares (the Roman Mars), he was boastful and belligerent and I don't think his mother liked him very much. He became the god of War. His sister was Eris, a nasty little girl who was always trying to cause trouble. In fact it was she who craftily stirred up a bitter quarrel between her mother and two of her aunts which was so bad it finally led to the Trojan War (as you will see later). Eris became the goddess of strife. The next child was Hephaestos who had quite an adventurous childhood, but that is the next story.

HEPHAESTUS (*ROMAN VULCAN*)

When Hephaestus was born he was such a weak and ugly looking baby that he embarrassed his mother Hera, the queen of heaven, so much that she threw him away. He fell from the very top of Olympus, the highest mountain in Greece where the gods used to live, down into the ocean. Luckily a kindly sea goddess named Thetis rescued him and took him to her home in an underwater grotto. It was here that Hephaestus first tried metal working. With the help of Thetis he made the first smithy and produced many useful and ornamental objects. One day Thetis met Hera who noticed an exquisite brooch that Thetis was wearing. Naturally, Hera wanted to know from where she had got such a lovely jewel. Thetis did not really want to tell her, but Hera insisted and on learning the source of the jewel she suddenly realised how clever her son was and instantly demanded that he should be returned to her in Olympus. On his return, Hera gave him his own workshop encouraging him to make beautiful things for her. She made a great fuss of him and even arranged for Aphrodite, the most beautiful of goddesses to be his bride, which incidentally Aphrodite was not too happy about; but Hera, queen of heaven, had to be obeyed. Of course Hephaestus was delighted.

He was so pleased with his mother that one day when Zeus and Hera were having an argument he interfered, really a very silly thing to do. He took his mother's side and spoke angrily to his father. Now one did not speak this way to Zeus who, in a fit of rage picked up Hephaestus and threw him off Olympus again. This time the poor fellow landed heavily on the ground at Lemnos breaking both his legs so badly that ever after he had to wear leg-supporters (callipers); these he made himself out of gold.

Hera missed the beautiful things that he made for her so much that she pleaded with Zeus to pardon her son, which eventually he did. Hephaestus returned to Olympus and became god of the Smiths.

ATHENE

In ancient biblical times men had many wives, like King Solomon, even today in certain parts of the world some men can have more than one wife and, of course, so had Zeus. He fell in love with a lady named Metis, who was a Titaness (I mentioned the Titans at the beginning). Metis was very wise and known as the Titaness of Wisdom. When Zeus found that Metis was going to have his child he consulted the oracle of Mother Earth and the answer caused him great anxiety. He was told that this would be girl child, which of course pleased him, but next was the bad news. If Metis had another child it would be a boy, now that of course sounds fine, but, and here is the snag, the boy would grow up to destroy his father and become Lord of the Heavens. Zeus was desperate, what could he do? Suddenly he remembered what his own father Cronus had done before and quickly grabbed hold of Metis with his powerful hands, opened his mouth and swallowed her whole. After doing this he just carried on as though nothing had happened and put the incident completely out of his mind.

Some months later he suddenly developed a terrible headache and it was driving him mad and he could stand the pain no longer. He told his son Hephaestus to place a wedge on top of his head and split it open with his heavy iron hammer. Hephaestus said to his father that surely that would kill him, Zeus told him not to be so silly because we are gods and cannot die. Hephaestus did as he was told and out of Zeus's head sprang the girl child of Metis, a little figure dressed in armour and fully armed. She rapidly grew to full size and shouted a terrifying battle cry. The split in the head of Zeus immediately healed and it ached no longer.

This child was Athene and as she was born fully armed she became a warrior goddess and protected all Greek soldiers who fought for the good of mankind. It is easy to see why she was also the goddess of wisdom, having been born from Zeus's head and her mother being the Titaness of Wisdom.

ARTEMIS AND APOLLO

Zeus fell in love with a beautiful and gentle lady named Leto and he made her one of his wives. Hera, who you remember was his first wife, was jealous and became furious when she found out that Leto would soon be giving birth. She ordered a huge serpent Python to chase and torment Leto thus making it impossible for her to rest anywhere to have her babies in comfort. In desperation Leto summoned up all her strength and ran as hard as she could behind a mountain and while Python was looking for her she slipped over to the island of Delos. Hiding herself away she quickly gave birth to a girl child named Artemis. (The children of the Olympian gods are certainly different to mortal children because Artemis immediately grew up and helped her mother give birth to another child). This time it was a boy, his name was Apollo and like his sister he grew up straight away. Hephaestus made Apollo a bow and arrows with which he went looking for Python his mother's enemy. Python saw Apollo coming and rushed in a panic to a sacred shrine at Delphi seeking sanctuary, the priests of this sacred area attempted to stop Apollo entering, but he roughly pushed them aside and finding Python cowering behind an altar raised his bow and arrow and shot Python dead. He had avenged his mother, but he had violated a religious area.

To atone for this transgression, Zeus commanded that he must instigate certain contests to be held every four years in memory of Python and these became known as the Pythian games. Apollo built a temple on the site and became the god of prophecy, and if you go to Delphi at the present time you can see the ruins of this temple.

Apollo appointed a priestess, known as a Sibyl and her job was to prophesy and give advice to any who came to ask for his help. The fame of the oracles given by the Sibyl quickly spread and people came from all over the then known world to have their fortunes told.

Even today some people consult fortune tellers and many read their horoscopes in the daily papers, all hoping for good luck, so the ritual started by Apollo has never died. Apollo was a very popular god and was always depicted as a good looking, athletic and healthy young man. After inventing the seven string lyre he became the god of music and as he was also the god of healing and of hunting it seems he must have been kept very busy.

Artemis, Apollo's sister, was also very popular as a goddess in the ancient Greek world. One day when she was sitting on her father's knee, as some children do, Zeus, her father, asked her if there was any particular present she would like. Artemis asked for a bow and arrows like her brother's as she loved hunting. Zeus granted her wish and she became the goddess of the hunt. When you see pictures or statues of her she is often accompanied by a hind or a dog. She spent her days hunting and when the chase was over she loved to sing and accompanied herself on the cithara, an ancient Greek instrument associated with the harp. Thus she became the goddess of music. She was also the goddess of prosperity which she was supposed to bring to those who honoured her.

HERMES, A GREEK GOD

Zeus, King of the Olympian Gods married many times and one of his wives was a lady called Maia, who gave birth to a boy they called Hermes. (The Romans called him Mercury). Hermes was a naughty little boy always up to mischief. He lived with his mother in a large cave, and one day when his mother was out climbed out of his cot and crawled out of the cave. He looked around to see just what mischief he could get up to when he spotted a herd of cows which belonged to the Greek god Apollo, who was half brother to Hermes (they both had the same father, but a different mother). The naughty Hermes decided to steal the cows!

He was very cunning in how he did this, because he stripped the bark off a tree, cutting it into pieces and tying the pieces on to the hooves of the cattle so that their hoofprints would not show on the ground. To make things more confusing, he pulled the cattle backwards by their tails, then hid them at the back of the cave.

Of course Apollo was angry when he saw that his beautiful cattle had been stolen and stormed around the countryside looking for them.

As he walked past the cave where Hermes lived he heard sounds of music coming from inside. 'That is very peculiar,' he thought, and looked inside; there he saw Hermes playing an instrument that he had just made.

"That is a fine instrument" said Apollo, "I've never seen one like that before", which as Hermes had only just invented it was hardly surprising. Apollo asked Hermes how it was made Hermes proudly explained that he had hollowed out a Tortoise shell and stretched cow gut across it. Apollo said that he could understand the tortoise shell, but where did the cow gut come from?

Then it suddenly dawned on him that it must have come from his own cattle.

"Have you stolen my cattle Hermes?" Apollo demanded in a loud voice. Hermes blushed guiltily, but denied that he had stolen the cattle.

It was then that the cattle hidden in the back of the cave started mooing loudly as they had not been fed. Apollo realised that they were indeed his cattle and told Hermes that he thought their father should hear about his tricks. Whereupon Apollo dragged Hermes off to see their father Zeus. Zeus, at first, could not believe that a son of his would do such a thing, although he was rather amused by the boy's artfulness. However, he said, "I am not going to interfere, you two must sort this out for yourselves".

Apollo took Hermes back to the cave and being the elder brother, bigger and stronger, he threatened to box Hermes ears.

"Please don't do that" Hermes said, "I will give you back your cattle, they are unharmed, I did look after them and I also sacrificed one of them as an offering to you gods, who are so kind and understanding, there is no doubt you are marvellous and wonderful gods." Well gods like flattery and Apollo was no exception "All right," he said, "but which gods did you sacrifice to?"

"All twelve" said Hermes.

"Twelve!" said Apollo, "there are only eleven, who is the twelfth"?

"I am your servant sir" Hermes replied cheekily.

Apollo then said "You are a saucy little devil; as you know I am the god of music, so if you let me have that instrument you have invented, I will forgive you and we will be friends again".

This was agreed and they both went off to see Zeus, their father, and tell him the story and that all was now well between them.

Zeus was then informed that Hermes wished to become one of the select members of the Olympian gods; the ones who had more power and influence than lesser gods and consequently received more offerings. "What do you want to be the god of?" enquired Zeus,

"I would rather like to be your messenger father" Hermes replied.

"I think that can arranged" said Zeus, "but first you must promise never to tell another lie, we just cannot have that as Olympian gods - so no more lies, OK?"

"Certainly", Hermes answered "although I cannot promise always to tell the whole truth".

Zeus smiled and said "You are very cunning, my boy! What I am going to do is make you the god of liars and also, because of the devious way you purloined your brother's cattle, I will make you the god of thieves, and when they need help it is to you they will turn. And now that you are my special messenger, I present you with the herald's staff, a rod with a white ribbon attached, as a sign that you must be given sanctuary whenever required. Also I present you with a round hat to keep off the rain and finally a pair of winged golden sandals to speed you on your way".

Because Hermes had much travelling to do in the course of his duties, he also became god of travellers, and when mortals died, it was Hermes who went and collected them to take them to the other world. He was always very gentle when he did this and quietly, tenderly and lovingly laid them to rest, taking away their cares and worries. It was then that he would give them great comfort and personally escort them on their journey to the next life. So you see that he did finally become a rather nice, considerate and understanding god.

DIONYSUS

All the ladies that Zeus fell in love with that you have read about so far were goddesses. Zeus, however, did marry some that were mortal. One of these was a beautiful princess called Selene, the daughter of King Cadmus of Thebes. Now Zeus could not really court a mortal in his true image of the mighty king of gods and men, so he disguised himself as a mortal man. Mind you he was, of course, an extremely handsome and charming young man. Selene could not refuse such an attractive suitor, not realising for one moment who the love of her life really was. Things went well between then and they were very happy together. However, Hera was not so happy, in fact she became extremely jealous and decided to get rid of Selene.

Being a goddess, of course, she could do all sorts of magical things and changing herself into the shape of one of Selene's friends went to visit her while Zeus was away. Hera managed to convince Selene that her charming lover was not so nice as he appeared and that he was really an Olympian god masquerading as a mortal purposely to deceive her. Selene at first could not believe what she had heard, but she was worried at the news. The next time Zeus came to her she asked him if what she had been told was true. Zeus admitted that it was, but refused to tell her which of the gods he was. Selene however insisted that he appear to her in his true form which, after

much arguing, he finally did. As he was so enraged at being found out he turned himself into thunder and lightning which struck Selene and of course killed her.
It so happened that Hermes was passing by at the time and was horrified to see the fate of poor Selene, especially as she was due to give birth in a few months time. He quickly removed the unborn baby from her and sewed it into Zeus's thigh where it was safe until the time came for it to be born; eventually the baby, a boy named Dionysus was born. You remember how Athene came from the head of Zeus and so Dionysus came from his thigh?

Zeus knew that Hera would be furious if she found out about Dionysus and would, no doubt, try to do something terrible to the boy, so he hurriedly brought the boy to earth and instructed King Athamas and Queen Ion of Orchomenus to hide him. This they did by putting him in the women's quarters where he was brought up by them. By the time Dionysus had passed his childhood Hera lost her hatred for the boy, however, she would not agree to him being allowed to live on Olympus with all the other gods until he had been sent round the world to further his education. He departed immediately and during the course of his travels discovered the fruit of the vine (grapes of course) and found that he could make wine from their juice. Wherever he went on his journey he taught men the art of wine making, finally bringing this art back to Greece. All the people were pleased with Dionysus because they enjoyed drinking wine so much (as indeed many people do to this day) that they made him the god of wine. Dionysus they said brought this gift to them. He became one of their favourite gods, at least until people drank too much and got headaches and I think that then sometimes they changed their minds.

PROMETHEUS

You have read of the way many of the Greek gods came into existence according to their mythology; here is one of their explanations of how mortals first came into the world. For this myth we must refer to my first story about the birth of the gods in which I mentioned the Titans. They married Titanesses and had many children who grew up to be strong and powerful giants. They banded together and conspired to overthrow the Olympian gods. This resulted in a fierce battle between the two sides with losses and gains for both. It really was a terrible battle: the Titans were so strong that they not only threw colossal boulders, but also tore huge trees out of the ground to use as weapons. Zeus hurled hundreds of thunderbolts at the Titans, the noise was deafening and the force of them was so enormous that they caused fires and even earthquakes!

The war lasted ten years and the outcome was doubtful until Athene threw a vast missile that crushed the Titans' leader. You can see just how huge this missile was by looking on a map, as today it has become known as the island of Sicily. To make their victory complete Poseidon, the god of the sea, broke off part of the island of Kos with his trident and with this he crushed Polybates who had taken over command of the Titans. Without their leaders the Titans surrendered and many of them were put in chains and cast into the depths of the earth.

Atlas, one of the Titans, was punished by being made to hold up the heavens on his powerful shoulders for eternity[1].

Prometheus the wisest of all the Titans, and his brother Epimetheus who was rather simple, escaped punishment, at least for the time being.

It was Prometheus who made the first man[2]. He made him out of clay in the image of the gods and got Athene to breathe life into him. At the same time he made all the animals. Now he entrusted his brother Epimetheus to issue to the animals all the qualities that they would need to live, such as great strength for some animals such as the lion, speed for others like the hare and the deer, and for birds the gift of flight. Epimetheus was rather scatterbrained and quickly used up all the desirable qualities on the animals leaving none for man. However, Prometheus himself bestowed on man the ability to talk.

Now man knew that he had to sacrifice to Zeus, but did not know how to go about it.

---

[1] *Eventually, after many years he was transformed into a mountain and it is still supposed that on him rests the sky and all its stars.*

[2] *It is important to remember that man in this context really means mankind or the human race.*

He asked Prometheus who told him to kill an ox and cut it open, then take all the fat, gristle and bones and change them over with all the nice juicy meaty parts, then sew the animal up. He was to ask Zeus which part he would like. Naturally Zeus chose what he thought was the tastiest part of the animal, but, of course, these parts had been changed around. You can imagine how livid Zeus was when he realised he had been tricked into accepting the parts man did not want. It was however too late for him to change his mind, but what he did do was to take away fire and with no fire the meat could not be cooked and man would have to eat his meat raw, which is not very pleasant.

Prometheus realised what had happened so he slipped into Olympus by a back door and breaking off a large fennel stick he hid a fragment of glowing coal inside and took it back to earth. Once there he blew on the hot cinder that was inside the fennel stick which immediately burst into flames and that was how man got back his fire.

Naturally Zeus soon found out that fire had been stolen from Olympus and was furious. He decided to punish both man and Prometheus. He had Prometheus arrested and imprisoned on a mountain, (you will be able to read what happened to him later in the story entitled "How the Trojan War Started"). To punish man he ordered Hephaestos to make a model of a woman and breathed life into her. The name of the lady was Pandora and she was the most beautiful woman in the world. Well she must have been because, after all, she was the only one! Zeus now offered her to Epimetheus to be his wife. Epimetheus was rather reluctant because his brother had warned him never to accept any presents from Zeus, but realising that Zeus would punish him if he refused he married Pandora. Epimetheus had a box his brother Prometheus had given him for safe keeping and had told him that it must never on any account be opened. Pandora knew about this box and it fascinated her, she just could not imagine what was inside. Perhaps it contained beautiful jewels which could be hers. Maybe it held something else even more precious. She could contain herself no longer! She thought that if she just opened the lid slightly and peeped in surely that could do no harm. Then with trembling hands she eased the lid up. As soon as she did this the lid suddenly forced itself completely open and out flew a swarm of horrid ugly looking creatures similar to great fat bluebottles only much worse. They buzzed and made nasty noises as they multiplied and then swarmed all over the earth. These pests are the evils that mankind suffers today such as sickness, plague, deceitfulness, old age etc.

Pandora quickly slammed down the lid, but it was too late. She did, however, manage to trap one creature inside the box and that one was "Hope". So no matter what troubles man suffers from these days there is always hope left.

MELAMPUS

This is the story of two brothers who grew up together and were deeply attached to each other. Their names were Melampus and Bias.

One day when they were out walking with their father they came across a snake in their path. Now Melampus loved all creatures and he was most upset when his father killed the snake, after all it had done them no harm. He gently picked it up and was stroking it when he suddenly heard a strange noise coming from nearby. Looking around he saw a nest of young snakes who seemed to be crying for their mother. He tenderly and reverently buried the snake and took its young under his care, thus he saved their lives and looked after them. Eventually, they grew up and were ready to lead their own lives, but before going off into the world they decided to reward Melampus for his kindness. When he was asleep they silently crept up to him and kissed his ears before they left. Now these kisses had a magical effect because when Melampus woke he found that he could understand the language of all animals and birds.

It so happened that Melampus's brother Bias had fallen in love with a beautiful princess who had many admirers. Her father promised her hand in marriage to whoever brought him the cattle of King Phylacus. These cattle were guarded by an unsleeping and unapproachable dog. As Melampus was so fond of his brother and understood the language of the animals, he said he would undertake to obtain the cattle for him. (It came to his knowledge that Phylacus would give his cattle to anyone who attempted to steal them, and was caught and locked up for exactly one year).

In the dead of night Melampus approached the cattle when the dog suddenly jumped out of hiding and cornered him and would not let him move until Phylacus arrived and led him away to prison. This is really what Melampus had planned to happen, but he knew that this must only last for one year for the prophecy to come true.

On the evening before the year ended, Melampus was sitting in his cell listening to woodworms chewing away at the wooden beams in the ceiling. All of a sudden one of them made a strange spluttering noise, of course Melampus could understand their language and he heard one of the woodworms say to himself "I had too much in my mouth and it went down the wrong way".

"Serves you right" said another woodworm, "you shouldn't be so greedy, I know this is a very tasty piece of wood and it will be finished by tomorrow".

"It will" said another, "if you shut up talking and get on with chewing".

Melampus immediately shouted for Phylacus and asked to be moved to another cell as this one was going to collapse in the morning. He was moved, even though Phylacus did not really believe him as the cell looked perfectly safe to him. When the prediction came true,

Phylacus was so impressed by Melampus's powers of prophecy he consulted him about an impediment from which his son, Iphiclus, suffered. He also told Melampus that if he could predict a cure he would willingly give him the cattle and his freedom. Melampus agreed and sacrificed two bulls to the gods and their carcasses attracted two vultures, which flew down from the sky and settled on the branch of a tree. The vultures started talking to each other and, of course, Melampus could understand every word they said.

"How nice to see you again" said one bird to the other.

"You too," said the second one, "Goodness its several years since we were last here and Iphiclus was only a little boy then, how time flies".

"That's right" said the other, "His father was performing an operation on some sheep with his knife. He went towards young Iphiclus with the knife, dripping with blood, still in his hand, and the boy took fright and ran away! Apparently he thought his father was going to do the same to him as he had done to the sheep! Phylacus hastily stuck the knife into an oak tree and ran after his son to comfort him. But, the shock left the boy with a fear of meeting strangers and he won't leave the safety of home".

"How sad", replied the other bird, "Especially as the cure is so simple. The knife is still stuck in the tree, if it was removed and rust scraped off it was mixed with wine and then drunk in doses for ten days the boy would be cured."

"Ah" said his friend, "We know this because we birds know many more things than human beings who, of course, think they are more intelligent than us, poor things".

As Melampus understood the birds, he was able to cure Iphiclus. He was given his freedom, and the cattle which, in turn, he gave to his brother, Bias, who was then able to marry the beautiful princess.

It is most important to remember that just because Melampus made friends with snakes and he knew how to handle them, it does not mean that you can do the same. In fact, in some cases it could be highly dangerous so leave them alone to live their own lives in peace and do not interfere.

PERSEUS

Acrisus, King of Argos was once told by the Oracle that he would be killed by his grandson. To forestall his fate he had his only daughter Danaë imprisoned in a tower guarded by ferocious dogs. Danaë was very sad. She would have loved to have gone to dances and meet others of her own age, played games and laughed with them as from the top of the tower she could see others doing. Zeus looked down from Olympus and feeling sorry for Danaë decided to pay her a visit. One day when Danaë was feeling more bored and unhappy than usual she saw a ray of golden light suddenly shine through the window. At first she though it was the sun reflecting on the glass, but then the shining ray turned into flakes of gold which fell on the floor. She watched in utter amazement as these golden flakes took shape and suddenly Zeus himself stood before her in the guise of a handsome young man wearing a beautiful golden suit. She thought she must be dreaming and pinched herself to make sure she was awake. Zeus told her who he really was and not to be afraid as he had come to marry her and bring some happiness into her life.

Danaë was overjoyed, she never thought for one moment that she would ever be married, and here was this charming and attractive young man proposing to her. Of course she agreed and Zeus regularly visited her after this, always secretly entering the tower disguised as a shower of gold. Nobody, not even her handmaidens had any idea of this marriage, so it was a complete surprise to everyone, especially the king, when Danaë gave birth to a baby boy she named Perseus. Acrisus was appalled, this infant was his grandson predicted by the Oracle to kill him. His immediate reaction was to kill both the boy and his daughter, which, somehow, he just could not do in cold blood.

He decided, however, that they must both be got rid of, so to ease his conscience he had the two placed in a small wooden box with a lid (like a Noah's ark) and cast into the sea where, out of his sight, he thought they would be drowned.

The box floated away and the weather suddenly became dark and cloudy, soon a storm blew up. The box was tossed this way and that and Danaë was very frightened, she knew she could not stay afloat for much longer and feared that soon they would be drowned. She prayed to Zeus for help and he hearing her prayers guided the box to the small island of Seriphos. A fisherman happened to be standing on the shore and pulled the box up on to the beach wondering whether he would find anything in it and, of course, he was amazed to find Danaë and Perseus. He took them to Polydectes, the king of the island, who gave them a home and they lived in the palace while Perseus was growing up.

During this time, Polydectes kept pestering Danaë to marry him which she firmly refused to do. He even tried to force her into marriage, but Perseus, who had grown into a powerful, strong and brave young man defended his mother. Polydectes was afraid of Perseus, but thought that if he could get rid of him Danaë would have no one to protect her. So he pretended he was going to marry another lady knowing it would please Perseus. Perseus was, in fact, so pleased that he asked Polydectes it there was any particular gift he could get for him as a wedding present.

He said "I will get you anything if you are not going to marry my mother, even the Gorgon Medusa's head" (Medusa was one of the three ugly sisters known as the Gorgons). As soon as Perseus had said this he could have bitten off his tongue, as he realised that it was a stupid thing to say because he did not really mean it.

Polydectes grinned, he knew that anyone who looked at Medusa was turned to stone, and, thinking to himself that Perseus was bound to perish in his attempt to tackle the impossible task of removing Medusa's head gave him no time to change his mind, he thanked him and said that it would be a most acceptable gift, far better than any other which had been offered.

Now it so happened that Athene, who hated Medusa, overheard this conversation and decided that she would help Perseus all she could. She appeared before him and warned him never to look Medusa in the face, only to look at her reflection. Athene then gave him a highly polished shield which shone like a mirror, she then persuaded Hermes to lend Perseus a sharp sickle and winged sandals and also a leather pouch in which to put the head of Medusa, finally Hermes gave Perseus a helmet which would make him invisible. Athene now instructed Perseus to search for three old hags known as the Graeae who had swanlike necks and only had one eye and one tooth which they shared between them. These creatures were the Gorgon's sisters and only they knew where the they could be found, somehow Perseus had to get this information. Perseus eventually found the Graeae sitting behind a mountain, silently he crawled along the ground towards them hardly daring to breathe in case they heard him. When he got close to them he quickly snatched away the eye and the tooth just as they were being passed from one sister to another. They screamed and demanded back the eye and the tooth, but Perseus refused to return them until they told him where the gorgons lived. After being told what he wanted to know he flew off with the aid of his winged sandals. Keeping the eye and the tooth with him.

    Suddenly in the distance he saw the petrified shapes of men who had been turned to stone by Medusa, and then he saw the three Gorgons sleeping peacefully using a rock for a pillow. Immediately he turned his head, knowing that if Medusa awoke and he saw her horrible face he would be turned to stone. On tiptoe he approached as near as he felt he could with safety, then turning his back on them he raised his polished shield and looking at their reflection in the shining surface he slowly backed towards them. All of a sudden Stheno, one of the Gorgons, who must have been dreaming gave a loud snore and turned over in her sleep, as she did so she flung out an arm and touched her sister Euryale. Perseus broke out in a cold sweat, if they woke and saw him he was finished! But, Euryale just gave a disgusted snort and went on sleeping. Relieved, Perseus crept nearer to Medusa, who had snakes on her head instead of hair and they suddenly started hissing. Realising it was now or never and still looking in the bright shield at Medusa's reflection Perseus gave a mighty sideways swipe with the sharp sickle, cut Medusa's head clean off and put it in the pouch which Hermes had provided! To his utter amazement a winged horse named Pegasus sprang from the neck of Medusa and flew away to the stables of Zeus.

The commotion woke the other two gorgons who attacked Perseus with their razor sharp claws and enormous teeth, but he put on the helmet that made him invisible and so was able to escape.

Perseus then flew back to the Graeae and returned their eye and tooth, leaving them he flew over the Libyan desert where some of Medusa's blood dropped on to the sand and turned into snakes, which are there to this day.

Continuing his journey Perseus flew over Joppa where Cepheus the Ethiopian king lived with this wife Cassiopea. They had a beautiful daughter named Andromeda who Cassiopea once boasted was more beautiful than the Nereids who were nymphs of the sea and the daughters of Poseidon. The Nereids could not believe that a mortal could make such an outrageous claim, a mere mortal more beautiful than they, and they were appalled! When they told their father, Poseidon, he was furious, so much so that he sent a huge sea monster to damage the coast and eat anyone he caught. The people lived in terror. After many prayers they consulted the Oracle and were told that the monster would only leave if Andromeda was given to him. Poor Andromeda was dragged to the sea, chained to a rock at the water's edge and left for the monster to devour!

Perseus, flying overhead, looked down and saw this beautiful young maiden with terror showing on her face and tears in her eyes desperately struggling to free herself from the chains. He fell in love with her at first sight and was determined to rescue her. Already it seemed too late as the monster had also seen Andromeda. It was rapidly swimming towards her with its huge mouth filled with many sharp pointed teeth open to bite her to pieces. As the monster raised its ugly head to strike, Perseus zoomed down from the sky and struck its head with his sharp sickle. Shaking its head, the monster turned to face the unexpected assailant. Seeing Perseus flying around above him, he let out a great roar and lashed the sea with his tail causing waves as high as a house! The great head shot forward at the speed of lightning trying to catch Perseus in its powerful jaws, but Perseus was even quicker and managed to thrust the pointed end of the sickle into the creatures neck. This really enraged the monster and it viciously continued to attack Perseus with renewed vigour, but it could not quite catch Perseus who would fly swiftly out of its reach and then swoop down like a falcon after its prey. At last he caught the monster off guard and using all his strength managed to cut its throat. The monster was killed and its body sank into the sea. Perseus quickly freed Andromeda from her chains and they fell into each others arms.

King Cepheus was so delighted that brave Perseus had saved his daughter and saved his kingdom from the monster that he was only too pleased to consent to their marriage. This was arranged straight away.

Now during the wedding feast an unhappy incident occurred. The king had previously promised his daughter's hand in marriage to someone else, one of their own countrymen named Phineus. Phineus was overcome with jealousy to think that a foreigner had arrived and stolen his intended bride, and with two hundred supporters he burst in among the wedding guests intending to kill Perseus! A fierce battle took place and Perseus was losing, in fact being greatly outnumbered he could not win. Averting his eyes he pulled the Gorgon's head from the pouch and held it high in the air above his attackers who seeing Medusa's face were immediately turned to stone. Perseus then flew off with Andromeda and took her to meet his mother Danaë.

Now you may remember that Polydectes had tried to force Danaë into marrying him and in a plan to get rid of Perseus he had pretended that he was going to marry someone else. When he had asked Perseus for the Gorgon's head as a wedding gift he had never for one moment believed that Perseus would return from what seemed an impossible task. Of course, when Perseus did return, Polydectes could hardly believe his eyes and demanded angrily "Have you brought my present, Medusa's head? Because if you have not fulfilled your promise, I will send my soldiers to fetch Danaë and force her to marry me".

Perseus then said "I can see you do not believe that I have the head with me, therefore, would you like to see it"?

"Show it to me" sneered Polydectes and Perseus immediately lifted the Gorgon Medusa's head from the pouch and when Polydectes saw it he turned to stone with the sneer still on his face.

At this moment, Athene suddenly appeared and took back from Perseus all the things he had been lent; she gave Hermes back his sharp sickle, the winged sandals, the leather pouch and the helmet of invisibility. Medusa's head she kept herself and put it on the front of her shield.

Now we return to Acrisus, Danaë's father, who had been told by the Oracle that his grandson would kill him. Some games were taking place and Acrisus took his seat in the stadium to watch. He did not know that his grandson Perseus was one of the competitors. Perseus had entered the discus throwing event and when it came to his turn threw the heavy discus so high that it looked as if he would be the winner. Everyone looked in amazement as the discus soared so high into the sky, then just as it started to return to earth there was a sudden gust of wind which blew the missile off course and it headed straight for Acrisus. As the sun was in Acrisus's eyes he did not see that this heavy object was heading straight at him and it hit him on the temple instantly killing him. This, of course, was an accident, but the prediction of the Oracle had come true. He had been killed by his own grandson.

BELLEROPHON

Bellerophon, who was a brave handsome young man came from a wealthy and important family and lived in Corinth with his parents. He was also an unlucky young man, because, quite by accident he had killed his friend. Frightened that no one would believe it was not his fault he ran away to another country. He found refuge with King Proetus of Tiryns, a family friend who had known and liked him ever since he was a little boy.

Unfortunately, Bellerophon was still unlucky because Anteia the king's wife fell in love with the handsome youth and told him so; she even suggested that they should run away together! Bellerophon was appalled and ashamed and told Anteia so in no uncertain terms. He would not run away with her and that he thought she was a nasty and deceitful woman and please not to bother him! Then, Anteia who was very spiteful told her husband, the king, a deliberate lie, that it was Bellerophon who had asked her to go away with him! Of course Proetus believed his wife and wanted to have Bellerophon executed.

There was, however, an unwritten law in ancient Greece that any guest must be protected by his host. Proetus, therefore, dared not risk vengeance from the gods by murdering Bellerophon while he was still under his roof, so he wrote a letter to King Iobates, the king of

Lycia, who was also Anteia's father and asked Bellerophon if he would kindly deliver it for him.

Bellerophon departed and arrived safely at the court of King Iobates who made him very welcome. When Iobates read the letter the expression on his face turned grim, for the message he read was "kill the bearer as soon as possible because he had tried to run away with my wife, your daughter - signed Proetus, King of Tiryns". Of course, Iobates realised that Bellerophon was a guest under his protection and he would bring about the wrath of the gods if he carried out Proetus' instruction, but he must manage it somehow for the honour of his family.

The next day he told Bellerophon that Proetus had written in his letter that he was a brave warrior and always ready to help others. Bellerophon nodded in agreement and replied that he was always looking for some thrilling adventure.

"In that case" said Iobates "I call upon you to carry out an errand of the utmost urgency and rid our country of a foul pest". He then went on to explain that there was a monster ravaging the countryside known as the Chimaera. It had a lion's head, a goat's body, a serpent's tail and it breathed fire. Not only cattle, but also people had been killed by the fierce flames that spurted from its mouth and all the crops had been set on fire. Bellerophon bravely accepted the challenge, but before he went in search of the Chimaera he consulted the oracle for guidance. He was told that to perform the task successfully he must first catch and tame the winged horse Pegasus.

You have heard in the story of Perseus of how Pegasus was born when Medusa was killed. Pegasus, of course, lived on Olympus but occasionally used to come down to earth to drink the fresh clear water of the fountain at Peirene in Corinth. Athene guided Bellerophon to this fountain and gave him a golden bridle to put on Pegasus as it would certainly be impossible to put any other kind of bridle on an immortal horse. When Pegasus came for a refreshing drink from the cool waters of the fountain, Bellerophon quietly walked up to him and gently patted his neck. Pegasus snorted, shook his head and stamped his hooves, and was just going to fly off back to Olympus when Bellerophon threw the golden bridle over his head. The horse at once became tame and allowed Bellerophon to sit on his back.

Gently Bellerophon dug his heels into the horse's flanks, the horse then spread his wings and soared into the air going whichever way Bellerophon wanted him to.

On they flew until Bellerophon spotted the Chimaera in the distance devouring the flesh of some poor animals. Sitting firmly on the back of Pegasus he swooped down and attacked the monster with his spear. The Chimera let out a fearful roar and scorching flames shot from its mouth, and Bellerophon had to withdraw quickly for fear of being burnt to death. He attacked again, but before he could get close enough to use his lance, the creatures hot flames drove him away. The situation seemed hopeless, when suddenly he had an idea and fixing a large lump of lead to the end of his lance he attacked again, and when the creature opened its mouth he thrust the lead inside. The Chimera's hot breath melted the lead turning it into molten liquid which trickled down into the stomach of the monster, and burning its inside caused the monster to roll over on its back, where it smouldered away until only a heap of ashes remained.

Naturally, Iobates was delighted that Bellerophon had rid his country of the terrible Chimera, although he had secretly thought that he would be killed performing this task.

Iobates sent him on more and more missions, thinking and hoping that he would not return alive. When Bellerophon kept returning in triumph, Iobates began to think that the gods were on his side and that perhaps Proetus may have been mistaken, so he confronted Bellerophon with the letter that he had received from Proetus and asked for an explanation. Bellerophon gave him a true account of the affair and Iobates realising the truth begged his forgiveness for doubting him and they became firm friends.

It is such a great pity that many people who achieve greatness in life become conceited, and Bellerophon was no exception. He thought that as Pegasus would take him anywhere he wanted to go at his command that he was superior to other mortals and he foolishly tried to ride Pegasus to Olympus where the gods lived. As you may have heard, pride goes before a fall! Zeus sent a gadfly to sting Pegasus which made the horse rear violently throwing Bellerophon off its back. He fell to earth, but luckily Bellerophon was not killed by the fall; he broke many bones and was never able to walk properly again. He now realised what a fool he had been and spent the rest of his days repenting his stupidity. He was so ashamed of himself that he avoided contact with his fellow men and eventually died in poverty and despair.

INTRODUCTION

to

THE STORY OF
JASON AND THE GOLDEN FLEECE

    Since ancient times men have sailed the seas searching for fortunes. In Turkey there was a place called Colchis (is now Georgia, in U.S.S.R.) where gold had been found. In those days sheep skins were used to pan for gold. Consequently, as they were used as a sieve to separate stones from gold some gold dust would get attached to the fleece giving it a golden colour.
    Naturally the discovery of gold attracted many visitors, some legitimate merchants and some pirates out for plunder. The story of Jason is based on one of these expeditions. The answer to whether he was a merchant or a pirate is perhaps hidden in this story which has been handed down to us from ancient times.

JASON AND THE GOLDEN FLEECE

A young boy named Jason was the son of Aeson, a king of the part of Greece called Thessaly. When the king died Jason should, of course, have come to the throne. However, he had a wicked uncle named Pelias who plotted to murder the boy but Jason managed to escape, and his uncle claimed the throne. Pelias was not a very nice man being arrogant, insolent, wicked and cruel. One day the oracle at Delphi prophesied that he would loose his throne to a man wearing only one sandal.

Jason when he reached manhood decided that he would demand the throne as he was the rightful king. He confronted Pelias who went pale, seeing that Jason wore only one sandal as he had been hidden and brought up on the mountains where men did not wear a sandal on their right foot because the sole of the leather sandal would slide, and when climbing they could get a better grip with the bare foot. (Another version of the story is that Jason lost a sandal when helping an old woman to cross a river). Pelias realised that he must somehow destroy Jason, however, he pretended to be pleased to see him and even offered him the throne.

He said very amicably in the course of conversation "My dear fellow, please tell me what you would do if the oracle predicted that one of your fellow citizens was destined to kill you?"

Without hesitation Jason replied that he would send him to fetch the Golden Fleece from Colchis. Then said Pelias "I will willingly give you the throne when you fetch the Golden Fleece for me, that is the task I set you".

Jason was taken aback, but according to Greek law he could not deny this service. Oh dear! what could he do? He needed help. He sent heralds all over Greece appealing to brave and adventurous young men who welcomed excitement and a challenge to assist him. There were many who answered the call.

Jason had a friend called Argus who was an expert carpenter and he asked him to build the largest seaworthy ship that he possibly could. Argus built a fifty oared boat, which meant, of course, that it had to have a crew of fifty. Jason chose his crew from the bravest and fittest of the volunteers. We do not know exactly who the fifty were, because in later times many wealthy Greeks who were not entitled to, claimed that they were descendants of the Argonauts (the name the crew became known by). This was considered to be one of the aristocratic classes with great prestige value. However, we do know that a man named Tiphys was in charge of steering the ship. Orpheus was there and entertained his companions on the long journey by playing the lyre and reciting poems. Heracles (the Roman Hercules), the strongest man in the world, together with his squire Hylas was there. Argus, who built the ship and had it named 'the Argo' after him.

Also the well known twins of mythology, Castor and

Polydeuces (the Roman Castor and Pollux, now stars in the sky) famous for their ability to wrestle and box; together with many princes of the ancient Greek aristocracy. And, of course, we must not forget Jason, who was captain of the ship.

Before they started their long journey, they called in at Afissos to fill their earthenware jars (called amphorae) with water from a spring. This water had special health giving properties. (Even today the water at Afissos is known for its purity and the spring Jason used has now been channelled for public use in the central square).

They set sail and the voyage started by first passing the mountains of Pelion, Ossa, Olympus and then Athos, until they came to their first port of call which was the island of Lemnos. This island was inhabited entirely by women. Some time in the past these ladies had insulted the goddess Aphrodite, which of course was very silly of them as Aphrodite made them smell horrible and when their husbands came home from work they just could not stand their wives' horrible aroma, which really was a terrible stench, so they deserted them for ladies in a different country. It certainly must have been bad, but I think that over the years this foul smell must have gradually disappeared. The Argonauts were the first men that the ladies of Lemnos had seen since they were deserted by their husbands and they made the Argonauts so welcome that they did not want to leave the island or the ladies. It was Heracles who eventually made them leave, reminding them of the important quest they had all sworn to carry out.

Reluctantly the Argonauts sailed away. They came to what is known as the Hellespont, the passage between the Sea of Marmara and the Mediterranean which was guarded by the Trojans who would not allow shipping through. However, under the cover of darkness and keeping as quiet as mice they managed to slip past, much to their relief!

The Argonauts realised that they would have to land soon to collect provisions as there really was not much room on the Argo to store cargo. They called at the land of the Dolionians, a friendly people. When they arrived the wedding of the king was in progress and they were generously invited to take part in the wedding feast. During the feast a neighbouring tribe of six handed giants attacked the guests, however, the Argonauts being skilled and brave warriors beat off the attack earning the gratitude of Cyzieus, the king, (and incidentally their dinner and the provisions they were given to take on their way). They sailed away with a good wind behind them and made fine progress until unfortunately Heracles broke his oar. Pulling into the river Chius, where Heracles sent his squire Hylas ashore to look for wood to make another oar. However, Hylas stupidly did not bother to look where he was going and got lost in this strange land.

When Hylas did not return to the Argo, Heracles was frantic with worry as he was greatly attached to his faithful servant, and declared that he would not leave without him. This resulted in so much time being wasted that Heracles and Hylas were left behind, the other Argonauts continuing the journey without them.

The next island they stopped at was called Bebrycos which was inhabited by some terrible people, they were powerfully built and behaved like wild animals. Their king Amycus insisted on a boxing match with all visitors. He would wear iron gloves and smash his fists into the face of his opponent until he killed him.

Polydeuces, who was the first person to master the art of boxing, took up the king's challenge. He knew how to duck, weave and sidestep rather than just stand toe to toe trying to knock his opponent to the ground. So Polydeuces with his skill managed to catch Amycus off guard and hit him with a blow so skilfully aimed it cracked his skull and killed the king. The people were so dumbfounded to see what had happened to their leader that the Argonauts were able to escape, which they certainly lost no time in doing.

Their next port of call was Salmydessus, on the western shore of the Black Sea (This is on the entrance of the Bosphorus which leads to what is now Istanbul). It so happened that here lived a famous seer called Phineus, who Jason knew could give him advice vital to his journey. Unfortunately for Phineus he had once been so accurate with his prophesies that he had offended the gods. It does not do to upset the gods because their revenge is always terrible. Phineus's punishment was that his eyesight was taken away; also whenever he tried to eat a meal some horrible looking large birds called Harpies would suddenly swoop down and snatch the food away, leaving a mess on the table.   Phineus agreed to help Jason if he would rid him of these monstrous Harpies. A feast was prepared and these large ugly birds suddenly descended to devour it, they did not realise that they would be attacked by two of the Argo's crew called Calais and Zetes, sons of the North Wind, who had the ability to fly. These two brothers, armed themselves with swords and being expert swordsmen put the Harpies to flight. They flew away in a panic and Phineus never encountered them again.

He was so relieved by this that he told Jason how he could pass safely through two large rocks which tended to clash together unpredictably. Jason had been very worried about these rocks as he had to pass them on his journey and there was every chance that they would crash together and crush the Argo and its crew.

Phineus's advice was that Jason must send a dove through first and if it passed through safely then the ship might follow. The Argonauts sailed away, the sea was calm and the weather clear so they were enjoying their trip. Suddenly in the distance they heard loud splashing noises and the weather suddenly became misty and cold. Two great rocks appeared before them, larger than three houses on top of each other. They had to sail between these two huge rocks, and as they watched, these rocks suddenly crashed together making a tremendous noise and sending colossal waves which almost capsized their boat.

The rocks then parted and Jason sent the dove to fly between them. It had just completed its journey when the rocks clashed together again catching one of the tail feathers of the dove. As the rocks started to part, Jason ordered his crew forward and to row harder than they had ever rowed in their lives before. The Argo sped forward, furiously the crew tugged on the oars, knowing their lives were at stake. Suddenly the rocks stopped parting and began to close in on them. Harder and harder they rowed and closer and closer came the rocks. Just as the rocks were about to crush them they gave a final desperate heave on the oars and the boat shot forward just as the huge rocks crashed together. So close were the sailors to disaster that the rocks just clipped the stern of the ship. They all breathed a sigh of relief and somewhat shaken by their lucky escape they continued on their journey. (I wonder if these rocks could have been ice bergs, do you think they might have been?)

The Argonauts sailed through the Black Sea (known in those days as the Euxine Sea) along the coast of Asia Minor. After more adventures they reached the island of Ares. On this island lived great flocks of birds known as Stymphalian birds, which have since become extinct. These birds flew over the Argo and bombarded it by dropping bronze plumes, some of the crew were wounded, although not seriously. Half of the crew started rowing while the remainder protected them with shields against which they clashed their swords to frighten the birds away. (About these birds. - Jason could have reached the island of Ares at the beginning of May at the time of the great spring migration of birds. Some of these birds were exhausted and attempted to rest on the Argo. Sailors are well known to be superstitious, or they were in those days, and a great flock of birds trying to alight on their ship could have caused them to panic).

Soon after this incident the Argonauts arrived at Colchis. They presented themselves to King Aeetes, the ruler of Colchis and keeper of the Golden Fleece. They explained that they had been commanded to collect the Golden Fleece and take it to Thessaly. Aeetes could see that the Argonauts meant business and that they were hard and seasoned expert fighting men. He realised that it would be unwise, considering their military strength, to refuse their request point blank. He must think of some plan and while he was thinking, his daughter Medea came forward to meet the visitors.

Jason was struck by the beauty and grace of this lady and spoke charming words to her. Medea, for her part, meeting Jason, this handsome prince from abroad, immediately fell in love with him. Aeetes now having had time to think insisted that before he part with the Golden Fleece, Jason would have to complete a test, a test which he thought would be impossible for anyone to pass.

Jason must plough a field with two bulls, which really does not sound too difficult for a strong man, does it? However, there was a snag; these bulls had been made by Hephaestus, the god of smiths; they were made of bronze and breathed fire like a dragon. After Jason had ploughed the field he then had to sow it with serpent's teeth. Medea gazing into Jason's eyes whispered that if he would take her with him in the Argo and make her his wife, she would help him perform this task by the use of some magic powers that had been given to her. Jason replied by swearing to Medea that he would be faithful to her forever. That night Medea secretly met Jason and gave him a flask filled with a special ointment. This Jason was to smear over his face and body and he would then be protected from the bulls' fiery breath. Next day, Jason yoked the bulls and was able to plough the field without harm from the flames breathed by the animals, protected as he was by the magic ointment.

The next task to complete the test was to sow the field with serpents' teeth. As soon as they were planted they immediately grew into vicious armed, horrible looking men who started fighting each other. Jason knew that very soon they would attack him and, as at this time he was defenceless, he would soon be killed. No sooner had he had this thought than the men suddenly stopped fighting each other and slowly turned towards Jason. He picked up a large stone and threw it in the midst of the armed warriors. A row broke out between them, each accusing the other of deliberately hurling a stone at him. This argument turned to fighting which was so fierce that they finally all killed one another.

Having completed his task Jason went to the king for his reward, but Aeetes had no intention of parting with the

Golden Fleece, and was indeed actively planning to burn the Argo and kill the Argonauts.

Again Medea came to their rescue. She secretly took Jason to where the Golden Fleece was hidden. It was guarded by a huge serpent, which she put to sleep by feeding it with some special herbs. Jason crept stealthily past the sleeping monster fearful of waking it and quickly took the Golden Fleece from the oak tree where it was hanging! Then the Argonauts together with Medea and their prize rushed down to the Argo and hurriedly sailed away. King Aeetes was furious and gave orders that his fastest ship should be launched, to chase these intruders, who were all to be executed when caught.

Although the Argonauts were rowing as fast as they could they were slowly being overtaken by Aeetes. They tried taking evasive action by changing course several times but to no avail, the pursuing ship finally came alongside. Once again Medea came to their rescue; she had forcibly taken her younger half-brother Apsyrtus along as a hostage and now she drew a knife from the folds of her dress and slew the boy. She then cut him into pieces which she threw into the sea. Aeetes ordered his men to stop rowing in order to collect the boy's limbs so that he could be given a proper burial and this allowed the Argonauts to escape.

Getting nearer home after their long and perilous journey they touched upon the island of Crete. This island was guarded by a bronze giant called Talos, a huge monster who walked round the island three times a day looking for invading ships. Any that came within reach he either set on fire with huge firebrands or sank them by pelting them with great rocks. Medea however knew he had one weak spot. In one heel was a vein that was sealed by a bronze pin, and putting him into a trance she was able to remove this pin. Out rushed the divine ichor, a colourless liquid serving him for blood, and so he died. (I rather think that Talos was really a volcano which kept erupting until it finally exhausted itself).

Leaving Crete the Argo was caught in a storm, but finally they reached Thessaly with the Golden Fleece safely on board. King Pelias, who had of course sent them on their journey had not expected to see them again and would not keep his part of the bargain and surrender the throne to Jason. After going through so much hardship and danger Jason was not going to give up easily. He and his companions planned to attack the king, but Medea promised to capture the city single handed. She told them that when the Argonauts saw a torch being waved from the palace roof, this would be a signal that Pelias was dead, the palace gates open and theirs for the taking.

Medea first made a hollow effigy of the goddess Artemis, then she put on ragged clothes and made herself up to look like an old lady. She went to Pelias and told him that the goddess Artemis, whose sacred model she carried, had given her the power to make him into a young man again. The king of course was delighted at the thought of regaining his youth and, as requested by

Medea, called for his daughters to assist. They were very dubious that Medea could perform this feat, so to prove her point Medea turned her back to all of them and quickly removed her make up so that it looked as though she had become young again before their eyes. She then took a very old ram and cut it into pieces which she boiled in a cauldron, at the same time muttering spells. Next she placed the pieces into the image of Artemis and low and behold a frisky young lamb appeared! (Of course she had secretly hidden the lamb in there earlier.) She now commanded the daughters to do the same with their father, cut him up and boil him in the cauldron. Alcestis, one of the daughters was not convinced and declined to take part in this dubious ritual, but her sisters being completely fooled by Medea's trick to kill their father did as she bid. Medea now told them that while they were waiting for the cauldron to boil they must go on to the palace roof with torches and invoke the moon which is associated with the goddess Artemis. Of course Medea had no intention of bringing Pelias back to life even if she could.

Jason seeing the torches in the distance realised that Pelias was dead and was thus able to enter the city and claim the throne without opposition. When the citizens realised what a terrible deed had been committed they turned against the conspirators and refused to have anything to do with Jason or Medea, in fact they banished them from the city.

Jason and Medea fled and finally settled in Corinth. Jason became a great friend of Creon, the king of Corinth, who as it happened had a beautiful daughter called Glauce. Jason was ambitious and knew that if he could marry Glauce he would eventually become king of Corinth; he also knew that Creon wanted a son-in-law to support and succeed him. If only Medea was not there! Of course he he was indebted to her for all her services, but no legal marriage was possible between a Greek and a foreigner, and Medea was looked upon as a barbarian from a distant, backward country. She was now an embarrassment to him, the people of Corinth would not accept her.

Medea herself knew that her beauty was beginning to fade and as she saw Jason and the beautiful princess Glauce becoming more and more friendly towards each other her devotion to Jason turned to hatred. Jason asked Creon for his daughter's hand in marriage to which the king instantly agreed and decreed that the wedding must take place straight away.

At the same time the king sent word to Medea that she must leave Corinth immediately. Medea pleaded with the King to allow her to stay a little longer in order to gather her belongings together and to make provision for her and Jason's two sons. Creon knew that Medea would somehow cause trouble if she were allowed to stay. He listened to her gentle pleading words and was sorry for her, but suddenly he felt his blood run cold when it struck him that underneath her calm exterior, she was hatching some diabolical plot. Medea reassured him that she could hardly cause trouble in just one day and promised to leave early next morning. The king agreed to this, but warned her that if she was still in Corinth when the sun rose she would be put to death.

Of course Medea had already planned what she was going to do. First she sent for her two young sons and gave them a beautiful coat adorned with wonderful jewels. This they were to give to Glauce as a wedding present. It was such a magnificent coat that Glauce could not resist trying it on. Then something terrible happened. As soon as she put the coat on it caught fire and the more she struggled trying to take the coat off the closer the coat stuck to her. Creon, her father, rushed to help her, but as soon as he touched the coat it stuck to him too and they both perished in the flames.

Jason escaped from the fire, which by now had spread to the palace. After all that he had been through he was now a broken man. He wandered miserably from place to place until he eventually returned to Corinth where he found his old ship the Argo sadly rotting on the beach. Jason wearily sat down beneath its prow to shade himself from the heat of the midday sun and day dreamed about the many adventures he and his comrades had shared aboard the vessel. Suddenly, without warning, the prow of his old ship broke off and dropped on Jason killing him outright.

Medea fled to Athens where she was treated hospitably by the Athenians and, cunningly using her charms, she so captivated Aegeus their king that he married her. We will meet her again in the story of Theseus.

THESEUS

Aegeus, King of Athens, was very unhappy, he desperately wanted a son but his wife was unable to bear him any children. In desperation, he divorced her and went to consult the oracle at Delphi seeking advice. The priestess forecast that if he was patient one day he would have a son, but in the meantime he must not drink wine.

On his way home he called at Corinth where he met Medea. He told her about his problem and she promised to procure him a son by magic if he gave her his solemn oath to shelter her if she ever needed refuge. This scheming woman is already deceiving Aegeus, she is planning to commit murder, as we have seen in the story of Jason, and intends to bind Aegeus so firmly to a promise that he will be unable to refuse. Aegeus continued his journey home and on his way stopped at Troezen just down the coast from Athens, to visit his friend Pittheus its king. Aegeus told his friend his problem about not having a son and how he had gone to Delphi where the oracle gave him some strange advice about not drinking wine. Now it so happened that Pittheus had a beautiful daughter called Aethra, who he hoped would one day give him a grandson. As the two friends sat chatting after their evening meal, Pittheus insisted that Aegeus drink some of his fine wine that he had kept for a special occasion. Aegeus drank deeply, little thinking of the prophecy not to drink wine until he was ready to have son. That night he married Aethra.

In the morning he told her that he must leave to go to his kingdom in Athens. Before I go, he told her, I will place my sword and sandals under a large rock; if you have a son, when he becomes strong enough to remove my sword, big enough to wear my sandals and take them from under the rock send him to me in Athens and one day he will become king. Aethra did have a child and called him Theseus.

As he grew up the boy everyday would try to move the rock where his father had put the sword and sandals, but it was so heavy he could not budge it an inch. Then one day, when he was sixteen years old, as he heaved the mighty stone, he suddenly felt it move slightly. He rested a moment and then, pushing with all his might, the rock suddenly rolled away revealing the sword and sandals. Breathlessly, he rushed to his mother to tell her what he had found. It was then that she told him that he must go to his father in Athens where he was the rightful heir to the kingdom.

Theseus was excited with this news and being an adventurous young man decided not to take the easy route by sea, but to go overland where he could perhaps rid the country of some robbers and ruffians who were causing much trouble to travellers.

His journey went quietly enough until he was approaching Epidaurus when he was suddenly confronted by a highwayman called Periphetes. This ruffian would bludgeon all passers by with a huge club. After a fierce struggle, Theseus managed to wrench the club from Periphetes' hand and killed him with it. From then onwards, he always carried this club with him as it was such a useful weapon.

His next adventure came on the Isthmus of the Peleponese where a really nasty man named Sinis lived. It was his practice to bend two pine trees to the ground and tie one of his victims legs to each, then he would let the trees go and as they shot into the air they would split the poor victim in two. Theseus wrestled with Sinis and after overpowering him, killed him in the same manner and then continued his journey.

When he reached a place called Crommyum, he found the people starving and in much distress. A mad, fierce, monstrous wild sow had killed some of them when they were working in the fields. Now they dare not leave their homes to plough the ground to grow food, as each time they attempted to they were savagely attacked. Brave Theseus boldly stood his ground when the beast attacked him and sidestepping at the last possible moment smashed his club on the sow's head. However, this did not kill her but, as she was badly stunned, Theseus was able to finish her off with his sword. You can imagine how grateful the people were, in fact they became some of his most loyal subjects when he eventually became king. However, Plutarch, a famous writer in ancient times, was puzzled why Theseus should go out of his way to kill a mere sow. He came to the conclusion that the wild sow was in fact a woman bandit, whose habits were so disgraceful that she was nicknamed "sow".

Following the cliff road along the coast Theseus met Sciron, his next opponent. Sciron used to sit on a rock in the middle of a narrow path high up on the cliff and would order passing travellers to wash his feet before he would allow them to pass. As soon as they bent down to carry out his order he would give them a hefty kick in the backside which sent them hurtling over the side of the cliff. They would finish up in the sea where a man eating turtle was waiting to devour them. Theseus certainly was not going to lower himself by washing a stranger's feet, instead he picked up Sciron and tossed him over the edge of the cliff into the sea where the turtle ate him.

Continuing his journey to Athens, Theseus came to Eleusis where Cercyon a powerful wrestler lived. Anyone who passed by would be challenged by him to a wrestling match and, as he was so strong, he was always able to crush them to death. Theseus, however, relied on skill rather than strength and had actually invented the art of wrestling. Seizing his opportunity when Cercyon was off guard, he grabbed him round the knees. This action toppled Cercyon over and as he fell he caught the back of his head against a boulder and was killed instantly.

Nearing Athens, Theseus came to the house of Procrustes and, as night was falling and he felt weary, he asked Procrustes for a night's lodging. Procrustes, grinning evilly, agreed to shelter Theseus providing he fitted exactly into the bed. Procrustes always insisted for the sake of neatness that his visitors must agree to fit perfectly in the bed. If they were too long he would chop off the bits that overlapped and if they were too short he would stretch them. Artfully, Theseus made Procrustes try the bed first, he did not fit, so Theseus gave him the same treatment he had given others. The next day, Theseus carried on to Athens.

Of course, as Theseus had grown up at Troezen his father Aegeus had no knowledge of him. It was during this period that Medea had to escape from Corinth and fleeing to Athens she made Aegeus keep his promise to look after her. He took her in and thinking that Medea would give him a son and heir by magic, as she had once said she would, he married her. Of course, he did not realise that he already had a son when Medea gave birth to a boy they called Medus. It was Medea who recognised Theseus when he arrived in Athens and she was extremely annoyed and jealous because her own son would no longer inherit the throne as she had planned, and she realised that somehow she must dispose of Theseus. Quickly she hatched a cunning plan. First, using all her charms, she persuaded Aegeus that this apparent stranger had come to spy for some foreign power planning to overthrow the kingdom. She suggested arranging a feast where Aegeus was to give Theseus a cup of wine that she had prepared. Of course she was going to poison the wine and if he gave it to Theseus it would result in him killing his own son.

At the feast Theseus was offered the cup of poisoned wine which he placed in front of him ready to drink during the meal. A large joint of meat was placed before him, for being the guest of honour etiquette demanded that he have a choice of the first cut. To perform this operation he drew his sword which Aegeus immediately recognised and realised that the boy was his son. Quickly picking up the wine Medea had poisoned, he dashed the cup to the ground. Medea went pale, she knew that her evil plot had been discovered. She and her son Medus were banished from Athens, never to return again.

There was great rejoicing in Athens over the arrival of Theseus and Aegeus shared his throne with his son. Later, we will meet Theseus again in the story of Minos and the Minotaur.

MINOS AND THE MINOTAUR

Many years ago Minos and his wife Pasiphae lived in the palace of Knossos where they ruled over the island of Crete. One day Minos prayed to the sea god Poseidon to send him a bull which he wanted for a sacrifice to the gods. His prayer was answered and a most beautiful bull emerged from the sea. Minos was so pleased with this wonderful animal that he did not keep his promise to sacrifice it, but substituted one of his own inferior bulls. This was a silly thing to do as it was obvious to the gods that he had broken his promise and they were very annoyed. To get their revenge, they arranged for Pasiphae to give birth to a monster which had a bulls head and a human body and was called the Minotaur. Minos was so ashamed of his offspring that he commanded Daedalus, an expert craftsman, to build a large and complex labyrinth or maze, the centre of which was to be the home of the Minotaur. Thus, this monster was hidden from the people and if anyone strayed into the labyrinth and the Minotaur did not kill and eat them they would still be unable to find their way out.

One of Minos' and Pasiphae's sons was Glaucus; he was really only a little boy and very inquisitive. Once when he was wandering around the palace he came across some storage jars These jars were very big, some even taller than a man, and they can still be seen at the palace of Knossos to this day. Somehow, Glaucus managed to climb to the top of one of these jars, but he lost his balance and fell in. This particular jar was full of liquid honey and consequently Glaucus was drowned. His mother and father were very worried when he did not appear for his afternoon tea. Usually he was there first waiting to tuck into the home made honey cakes and other sweetmeats, so naturally they felt something was wrong.

King Minos called for Polyeidos, the court physician, and commanded him to search for the boy. Polyeidos discovered Glaucus and reported to the king what had happened. Minos replied that he must return and cure Glaucus. Polyeidos protested that this was impossible as the boy was already dead. Minos shouted at him "I employ you as a physician for my family and I pay you a lot of money, go and cure the boy immediately and earn your wages. You will be locked up with him until you do, locked up for ever if necessary".

Polyeidos was certainly not very happy, there he was imprisoned with Glaucus and absolutely nothing he could do about it. He glanced round in the half darkness and saw a snake slowly wriggling across the floor. Picking up his staff he attacked the snake and giving it a mighty whack on the head killed it. He sat down again and was just nodding off to sleep when he suddenly noticed another snake slithering across the floor. This reptile seeing that its mate was dead quickly shot back to a hole in the wall and disappeared. Then, all of a sudden, it returned carrying some herbs in its mouth. These it dropped into the mouth of the dead snake which immediately came to life and they both wriggled away quite happily together. Polyeidos was amazed, he picked up some of the herbs that had been dropped on the floor to see what kind they were. He was puzzled as he had never seen any like these before. Then an idea struck him. If the herbs worked for the snake, why would they not for Glaucus? With great care he forced the remaining herbs into the dead boy's mouth. Sure enough, Glaucus started breathing again, then he opened his eyes, he had come back to life.

Of course the king and queen were absolutely delighted and rewarded Polyeidos handsomely and his fame spread all over the country. Even today the badge worn by the medical branch of the armed services, which represents a symbol of healing, is the staff of Polyeidos together with two snakes.

Glaucus had an elder brother called Androgeos who was a fantastic athlete. In fact, when he went to Athens and took part in the Athenian games he won every contest. In those days there was no second or third prize, it was the first that counted. Aegeus, king of Athens, was extremely annoyed to see a competitor from a small country like Crete beating all his finest athletes. He was so upset at all the valuable prizes being taken from Athens that he arranged for Androgeos to be waylaid on his way home, robbed of all his prizes and then killed.

When Minos found out what had happened to his son, he prayed to Zeus for revenge. Zeus answered his prayers by causing great famine in Athens. The people were starving and a deputation was sent to consult the oracle at Delphi for advice. They were then told that the famine would continue until they gave Minos whatever satisfaction he might ask for. A messenger was sent to Crete and Minos told him that seven youths and seven maidens must be sent every year to be given to the Minotaur while this monster was still alive.

Two years have now elapsed and twice the youths and maidens have been sent to Crete never to return or even be heard of again. Now, once more we meet Theseus. You remember in the last story we left him after a happy reunion with his father, King Aegeus. When he heard about the tribute of youths and maidens that were now due to be sent to Minos, he told his father he was going to go with them. His father did not like the idea at all and did his best to stop him, but brave Theseus insisted.

Reluctantly, Aegeus agreed on condition that he sail away with a black sail and, if his mission of slaying the Minotaur was successful he must return using a white sail. This he would be able to see from a long way off and know that he need no longer worry about the fate of his son.

Theseus departed with the youths and maidens and finally arrived at Crete. That evening they were all invited to a banquet to meet Minos and his family. At the meal Ariadne, a daughter of Minos, sat next to Theseus. She could not take her eyes off this handsome prince from Athens and knew she was falling in love with him. She also felt convinced that he had similar feelings towards her. Taking hold of his hand she whispered that she would help him kill the Minotaur and escape from the maze if he would take her to Athens where they could be married. Theseus did not really want to get married, but Ariadne was beautiful and he certainly needed help to get out of the labyrinth from which no one had yet escaped. With these thoughts in mind he agreed to her proposal.

When nobody was looking Ariadne passed him a sword, which he hid under his coat, then she secretly gave him a reel of thread. When the time came for him to enter the labyrinth he tied one end of the thread to a bush and as he went deeper into the complicated maze he unwound the thread. With the aid of the sword Ariadne had given him he was able to kill the Minotaur and found his way out of the maze by re-winding the thread which led him back to the entrance. Once out, he took Ariadne by the hand, rushed to his boat and with the other Athenians quickly sailed away before Minos realised what had happened. They stopped at the island of Naxos where they went ashore to replenish their supplies of food and water. After they had set sail again, it was soon realised by the crew that Ariadne was missing. Theseus had left her behind!

It could be that he had left her behind on purpose because he refused to turn the ship round to go back and collect her; perhaps he had changed his mind about marrying her. On the other hand, it may have been the god Dionysus who deliberately made him forget her, because this god had fallen in love with Ariadne and as soon as Theseus left the island he visited it and married her.

Now Theseus is supposed to have forgotten to change the sail from black to the white one. Everyday Aegeus peered out to sea anxiously looking for a white sail to appear on the horizon. Eventually after weeks of waiting he saw a speck in the distance, too far away to make out what it was. As it gradually came nearer, he could see by its outline that it was a ship. At last his son has returned; the ship slowly draws nearer and, horror of horrors, he can clearly see the sail and it is black.[3] The effect of the shock of thinking his son was dead caused Aegeus to lose his balance and topple into the sea where he drowned. Ever since that time the sea has been called the Aegean after him.

At the death of his father Theseus became king. He ruled well and was popular with his subjects and the people lived in peace for many years to come.

---

[3] *Now personally I do not really believe that Theseus did forget to change the sail. As today in Piraeus, the port of Athens, some fishermen use dark red sails, and I think Theseus in place of the black sail raised one that colour, which was the usual one. Thus when Aegeus stood looking out to sea the sail in the distance would appear black, particularly as he would have had the sun in his eyes.*

THE END OF MINOS

Let us now return to Crete and King Minos before we see what happens to Theseus.

Minos is naturally extremely angry with Theseus, after all he not only killed the Minotaur he had also run off with one of his daughters and on top of all this he has another big setback. Daedalus that ingenious craftsman who made such wonderful things for the king, had literally flown away. Daedalus knew that Minos would never let him return to his home in Athens and that he and his son Icarus, who was with him, would forever be kept in Crete as prisoners at the king's beck and call. He told his son Icarus to collect any eagles' feathers that he saw lying about, which he dutifully did. When sufficient had been collected for his purpose he fixed them with wax on to a frame made of reeds and thus made two pairs of wings. One pair for Icarus and one for himself. These they strapped to their arms and then they climbed to the highest point in Crete from where they jumped into the wind and rapidly flapping their wings soared away. To young Icarus it was such a wonderful feeling to fly, so exhilarating. It really was great fun, he swooped down to the sea and flew low over the waves, which incidentally he had been told not to do in case the spray clogged the wings, then he soared upwards, turned and dived on passing ships. He really was having great fun, but the silly boy became over confident and decided to fly higher than the eagles themselves. The nearer he got to the sun, the hotter it got and consequently the intense heat melted the wax which held the feathers together and Icarus dropped like a stone and drowned in the sea. Where he perished is still called the Icarian sea. His father, however, flew on and landed safely in Sicily where the king, Cocalus by name, welcomed him with open arms.

Meanwhile Minos had set out on a ship to search for Daedalus. He knew that whoever Daedalus asked for sanctuary would not want him to leave and no doubt would pretend not to have seen him. Now Minos knew that Daedalus liked a challenge and could not resist solving puzzles. At all the places he called he would produce a large spiral conch shell and offer his host a large reward if he could thread it. This seemed an impossible task and none could do it. Eventually he landed in Sicily where he was entertained by Cocalus. During dinner Daedalus casually produced the shell saying he had challenged many to thread it, but they had all agreed it was an impossible task. Cocalus grinned and boastfully said that nothing was impossible for him. Taking the shell he excused himself from the table and took it to Daedalus requesting him to solve the puzzle. Daedalus thought for a moment and then suddenly the answer struck him. First he melted some honey and poured it carefully into the hole at one end of the shell. Next he took an ant and tied some thread to it. He placed the ant at the opposite end to the hole where he had put the honey. The ant crawled up and down the spiral curves until it reached the other end to get at the sweet honey. Of course as it did this it pulled the thread with it, thus the threading of the shell was completed by the ant. (I hope that Daedalus let the ant have a good feed of honey and did not tread on it. Don't you?)

The king triumphantly took the threaded shell to Minos and claimed the reward. Of course, Minos realised straight away that it could only have been Daedalus who had the brains to solve this problem. He presented the reward to Cocalus but insisted that Daedalus be returned to him. This was agreed apparently amicably, but Cocalus had really no intention of losing this master craftsman.

He ordered his three daughters to prepare an evening bath for his guest. Then when Minos lay in the relaxing, scented warmth of the bath, the girls suddenly poured jars of boiling, scalding water over him and he perished. His body was returned to the Cretans who were told that he had tripped over a carpet and fallen into a cauldron of boiling water. But we know what really happened, don't we? Let us now see how Theseus is getting on.

THESEUS VISITS THE UNDERWORLD

We left Theseus after he had become King of Athens and united all the settlements of that area. The people were happy and peace reigned for quite a long time. (In fact this really did happen and Athens became a political centre of the part of Greece known as Attica, so this is one of the many examples where myth comes close to history.)

But the time did come when Theseus had to face serious war. Attica was invaded by the Amazons, a tribe of fierce women who spent all their time hunting and fighting and, like men, rode into battle on horseback. Hippolyta (Hippolyte) their queen placed her army on the Areopagus, the hill of Ares. (This was where St Paul later preached a sermon in Athens.) Fierce fighting took place and after four months when neither side had gained a decisive victory an armistice was called for. The two leaders, Hippolyta and Theseus, met to discuss peace terms. As they had so much regard and respect for each other as great leaders, it is perhaps not surprising that when they eventually came face to face they both fell in love. Peace was restored and Hippolyta and Theseus became man and wife. (In another version it was Antiope, Hippolyta's sister, who married Theseus, but I do not think so because the son they had was obviously named after his mother and was called Hippolytus).

When Hippolyta died, Theseus married Phaedra (She was the sister of Ariadne who, you may remember, Theseus took away from Crete and then left on the island of Naxos). They had not been married long when Theseus left her for quite a long time on her own while he went on an adventure trip with his faithful friend Peirithous. Peirithous's great ambition was to visit the underworld and bring back for himself Persephone, the daughter of Demeter (the goddess of vegetation), whom Hades the king of the underworld had abducted, and Theseus agreed to go with him. They found their way to the underground river Styx which they had to cross to get to Hades' kingdom. They bribed Charon the ferryman to take them across; on landing they were confronted by Cerberus, a fierce dog, a truly vicious hound of hell, they threw honey cakes to him and as he greedily gulped them down they slipped past this horrible animal. Finally they found Hades who was somewhat amused at their audacity, but greeted them kindly. He told them to sit and make themselves comfortable, as comfortable as possible, he said, as they would be there for a long time: in fact forever! As soon as Theseus and Peirithous sat in the two comfortable looking chairs strange things started to happen. The arms and sides of the chairs closed round them and they could not move no matter how much they struggled. In fact, they seemed to melt into their seats and actually became part of the chairs.

They were stuck there for many years until one day Heracles visited Hades. He was so saddened at the pitiful sight of these two poor men that he asked Hades to release them. Hades refused but allowed Heracles to try freeing them himself. Heracles tugged and tugged away at Theseus using every ounce of his mighty strength, suddenly there was a loud ripping noise as Theseus was torn free. So firmly had he been stuck to the chair that he left part of his flesh behind. That is why all Athenian descendants of Theseus are now supposed to have extra small backsides, but I must admit that this is something I have never noticed in all my visits to Athens. Theseus was now free, but poor Peirithous was left behind, because they just could not get him off the chair and, as far as I know, he is still there.

While Theseus had been away his wife, Phaedra, had fallen in love with Hippolytus who, being a very nice and honest young man, would have nothing to do with her. This made Phaedra very angry and in a rage she wrote a letter to Theseus saying that Hippolytus had been very bad and had insulted and shamed her so much she no longer wanted to live. Then she hanged herself. Of course, Theseus read the letter and thought that Hippolytus was the guilty party and banished him from Athens. He then prayed to Poseidon, the god of the sea, to rid him of Hippolytus. Poseidon answered his prayer by sending a huge wave out of the sea ridden by a white sea monster. As Hippolytus was driving his chariot along the coast road from Athens to Troezen he was suddenly confronted by this huge apparition. The horses panicked and the chariot was overturned dragging Hippolytus to his death. Theseus discovered the truth from the goddess Artemis, but it was too late to save poor Hippolytus. Theseus was very sad and decided that he needed to get away for a holiday to help overcome his sorrow.

He owned an estate on the island of Skyros where Lycomedes was king and as he had always had a friendly relationship with Lycomedes he decided to go there. Lycomedes greeted Theseus courteously and listened to his sad story. However, the king was actually jealous of the great fame and power of Theseus and when Theseus told him that he was thinking of leaving Athens permanently and retiring to his estate on Skyros, Lycomedes became worried. His great fear was that once Theseus was settled he would want to become ruler of Skyros himself. Lycomedes took Theseus on a tour of the estate to show him its boundaries and on this pretext he took him to the top of a high cliff ostensibly to give him a clear view of his property. It was then that he suddenly pushed Theseus over the side and he fell to his death. Theseus was buried at Skyros where his body lay for many years.

In the 5th century BC, Cimon, a famous Athenian general captured the island and took the bones of Theseus back to Athens where they were placed in the sacred enclosure of the Theseum, which is a temple close to the Agora at the base of the Areopagus.

HOW THE TROJAN WAR STARTED

Priam, King of Troy, was a good and popular king and together with his wife Hecuba lived a contented and peaceful life. They had several children, the eldest was named Hector who grew up to be tall, powerful and brave and later became Commander-in-Chief of the Trojan army and a famous warrior, feared by his enemies and loved by his men. Hector had a younger brother named Paris. When Paris was born the oracle at Delphi prophesied that if he was allowed to live he would be the cause of the destruction of the Trojan people.

At Delphi there was a sacred temple belonging to Apollo, who was one of the most popular of Greek gods. He was worshipped as the god of music, healing and hunting, as well as the god of prophesy; which all must have kept him very busy, don't you think? It was at Delphi that Apollo's priestesses, who were called Sybils, predicted the fate of Troy if Paris was allowed to live. Naturally this caused great worry and concern to his mother and father, King Priam and Queen Hecuba, who after much thought and heartache finally agreed, for the sake of Troy and the Trojan people, that Paris should not be allowed to live. A faithful servant was then summoned and given orders to take the infant Paris away to the hills and there kill him. When the servant had reached a lonely spot, he put Paris on the ground and pulled out a razor sharp knife. Just as he was about to plunge it into the baby's heart the little child opened his eyes and smiled at the man. A lump came into the servant's throat and he ran away with tears in his eyes, he just could not kill this innocent child. Eventually he stopped running and with tears still blinding his eyes he somehow managed to kill a wild dog and cut out its tongue. This he presented to the king and queen, telling them that this was the tongue of Paris and proof that he had been killed.

As you know all babies often cry and Paris was no exception; his crying was heard by a passing shepherd who consequently discovered the child. Now the shepherd and his wife desperately wanted a child, but up to then had not had one, so the shepherd finding the child thought that the gods had at last answered his prayers and sent him a son. When the man presented the child to his wife, she too was overcome with joy and taking the boy into her arms kissed and cuddled him. Young Paris was brought up as their own son and, in fact, actually believed that they were his natural parents so that when the shepherd grew too old to work, it was Paris who took over the job of looking after the flock of sheep. The knowledge that he really was a Prince of Troy would certainly never have entered his head.

We must now leave Paris minding his sheep and turn our attention to another of the Greek gods named Zeus.

Zeus was the king of the gods and at this time was seeking a wife, but had not yet made up his mind who he would choose. While he was thinking about his choice, the Delphic oracle issued another warning forecast which rather upset him.

The prediction was that there was a certain lady somewhere who, if she married and had a son, the son would be greater and more powerful than his father. Unfortunately, the oracle did not say who the lady in question was. Naturally, this was extremely worrying for Zeus, after all if he or one of the other gods married this mysterious lady, the son she probably would have would be greater and more powerful than any of them, and there was no way he could have that. Somehow he must find out who the mysterious lady was. He consulted the oracle at Delphi, but either it could not or would not tell him what he so desperately wanted to know. However, the priestesses did inform him that there was someone who knew the identity of the lady in question and that only he could reveal the name to Zeus.

It was unfortunate for Zeus that the knowledge had been given to Prometheus, one of his old enemies. Prometheus was one of the giant Titans who had made war against the Olympian gods and Zeus had punished him by condemning him to be chained on a mountain. Every day a large bird would peck out his liver and in the cold of night, as he shivered on the mountain, his liver would grow again for the bird to devour again the next day. This happened day in and day out and, as you can imagine, was very painful. Although Zeus pleaded with Prometheus to tell him who the lady was it was hardly surprising that he would not help him. Finally, Zeus reluctantly promised to set Prometheus free from his torture in return for the information he required and this was agreed. With great relief Zeus found out that the name of the lady was Thetis, one of the sea nymphs. Immediately, he decided that Thetis must marry a mortal man as quickly as possible. After all it didn't matter if a mortal was greater and more powerful than his father, he would still only be a mortal and no threat to the immortal gods.

Zeus chose King Peleus, a wise, wealthy and courageous man, a ruler loved by his people. Now Thetis, being one of the immortals, certainly hated the idea of having to lower herself to marry a mere mortal and protested strongly. Zeus, however, insisted and the wedding was arranged. All the gods and goddesses were celebrating at the wedding apart from one, Eris the goddess of strife, who was extremely annoyed because she had not been invited.

However, she did attend the reception, keeping out of sight of the revellers. Seeing Peleus (the groom) in the distance, she beckoned to him and when he came to see what she wanted gave him a golden apple with instructions that he must present it to the goddess who most deserved it. Eris pointed out three goddesses standing talking together and told him that he must offer the apple to them and they would decide to which one of them it should belong .

The ladies in question were Hera (Queen of the goddesses), Athene (goddess of wisdom) and Aphrodite (goddess of love). Printed on the golden apple that Peleus proffered was the inscription 'For the fairest'; now each of the goddesses thought that she was the fairest and they quarrelled over who should have the apple. After much argument they asked Zeus to decide, but he refused knowing that he would upset the two who did not receive the award. Zeus thought hard and finally decided that the wisest solution would be to appoint a mortal to be the arbiter. The mortal man he chose was Paris!

Paris was tending his sheep in the fields when he was suddenly confronted by Hermes, who was Zeus' messenger. Paris was startled and rather frightened by the appearance of the god, especially as he was accompanied by Hera, Athene and Aphrodite. Hermes gave Paris the golden apple and told him that Zeus commanded that he must decide which of the three goddesses was the fairest and give the golden apple to the one he chose.

Aphrodite who was standing close to Paris whispered into to his ear that if he gave her the apple she would arrange that he married Helen, the most beautiful woman in the world. "But surely" said Paris "she is married already".

Aphrodite replied, "do not worry I will use the powers vested in me as a goddess to arrange your marriage to her" Paris selfishly thinking only of himself gave her the apple little thinking or caring about the tragic consequences this act might, and in fact did, cause. Aphrodite now had to keep her part of the bargain. First she arranged for Paris to be reunited with his parents who, having thought that he was dead, were so pleased to see him that there was no way they would think again of having him killed.

They made him an ambassador and sent him to Sparta and it was there that he met Helen, and Aphrodite commanded her young son, Eros, to shoot some of his magical arrows into her. These arrows, which although they could not be felt, made whoever they hit fall deeply in love. Paris and Helen now very much in love eloped and fled to Troy. This was the cause of the Trojan war, as Menelaus, who was Helen's husband and king of the Spartan Greeks, loved her and was determined to get her back. He consulted his younger brother, Agamemnon, the king of the Mycenaean Greeks and together they raised an army and attacked Troy laying siege to the city.

At this point we will return to Thetis, the beautiful sea nymph and Peleus, the mortal man she was forced to marry. You may remember that the oracle at Delphi had predicted that Thetis would have a son greater than his father. She did have a son and his name was Achilles. Now Achilles father was a mortal man, so naturally Achilles was also a mortal man. But, Thetis loved her son so much that she wanted to make him immortal like the gods, therefore, she attempted to do this by putting him into a fire and burning off his mortal flesh (I think this would have certainly made him immortal as she would have burnt him to death!) However, Peleus seeing what was happening to his son, rushed over in a panic and pulled him out of the fire by his heel.

Thus Achilles was immortal all over except for his heel. (Some say that Thetis, holding him by his heel, plunged him into the river Styx to make him immortal). I think it is rather strange and I wonder why, if he was immortal all over and therefore invulnerable apart from his heel, he always carried a shield into battle to protect his body?

Achilles was finally killed, when Paris shot an arrow at him which pierced his heel, the only place where he could be mortally wounded.

Another strange fact is that Paris used arrows which had been dipped in poison, so was it a coincidence that the arrow hit his heel or would the poisoned arrow have killed him if it had pierced another part of his body?

We now return to the Trojan war which had been going on for ten years. The Greeks were beginning to doubt that they would ever be able to defeat the Trojans. It was then that Odysseus, one of the Greek generals, hatched a cunning plan. He designed and supervised the building of a large wooden horse, almost as tall as a house. It was hollow so that some of the Greek soldiers could hide inside. That night they left the model horse, with some of their best warriors secreted inside it, in front of the gates of Troy and the rest of the army pretended to sail away. The Trojans, thinking that the Greeks had left for home, were absolutely delighted. They felt that the wooden horse must be an offering to the gods and pulled it into the city.

That night they celebrated with much feasting, drinking and dancing, until finally thoroughly exhausted they all went to sleep. It was then that the Greeks who were hidden inside the hollow wooden horse opened a secret trap door.

They crept out silently, as quiet as mice, so that they wouldn't wake the sleeping Trojans, and then unbarred the gates of Troy letting in the rest of the Greek army which had returned under the cover of darkness. The Trojans were defenceless against this sudden surprising attack. The town was ransacked, burnt to the ground and most of its inhabitants were mercilessly slaughtered. Helen, however, was saved and reunited with Menelaus who loved her so much he forgave her for deserting him. He took her home to Sparta where they lived very happily together for the rest of their lives.

Troy had been destroyed all because Paris had taken the beautiful Helen and refused to return her to her rightful husband, King Menelaus. Thus the Delphic oracle had been correct in its prediction that if Paris was allowed to live, he would be responsible for the destruction of Troy.

ORPHEUS AND EURYDICE
(A Tale of Love & Tragedy)

Some people say that the Thracian King Oeagrus was the father of Orpheus, probably because the boy was brought up in Thrace across the northern borders of Greece. Thrace was famous for its poets. But, as Orpheus was such a marvellous musician others think that Apollo, the god of music, was his father. However, they all agree that Calliope, the Muse of epic poetry and the first in rank among her sister Muses, was his mother. Be that as it may, he grew up to be the most famous and talented poet who has ever lived. He had such a beautiful voice that when he sang and played his lyre (an ancient stringed instrument, similar to a harp) not only were people enchanted, but wild and savage beasts would come running to listen to him, mesmerised by his melodious music. What is even more amazing is that stones and rocks would sway in time to his music and trees would uproot themselves and dance. In fact, if you go to Thrace keep a look out for ancient oak trees on the mountains that still stand where they stopped dancing after Orpheus had finished playing. As you look closely at them it is easy to imagine them dancing. Now trees, especially oak trees have nymphs living in them and these creatures are known as dryads.

It was a beautiful summer's day when Orpheus sat under the shade on an oak and started to sing and play on his lyre. Eurydice, the nymph of the tree was fast asleep, but the sound of his delightful music wakened her. Orpheus saw the tree's branches rustling when to his astonishment the beautiful Eurydice slowly emerged from inside the tree. He stopped playing, his eyes wide open with astonishment, there in front of him was the most delightful and attractive young lady he had ever seen.

He took her in his arms and tenderly kissed her cheek. He had fallen head over heels in love with her as indeed she had with him. From that time on they met regularly and their love for each other grew stronger and stronger until eventually they made plans to marry. The wedding was such a wonderfully happy occasion and they knew that they would always live happily in perfect harmony together. Oh! how happy they were now. Unfortunately, we do not know how the present will appear in the future.

Watching the happy couple was Aristaeus a satyr, the brother of Pan. Satyrs are woodland creatures, followers of Dionysus the god of wine. They are naughty and mischievous and their behaviour could be compared to monkeys and goats, they have two small horns on their head, pointed ears, a very hairy body and legs like a horse with cloven hooves. As Aristaeus gazed upon Eurydice he felt a desperate urge to hug and kiss her.

Eurydice had been dancing every dance and feeling tired she left the revellers and sat on a fallen tree to rest for a while. Aristaeus saw his chance and with a shout of glee he rushed up to Eurydice and attempted to grab her in his arms. Startled by his shout, Eurydice guessing the Satyr's intentions ran off in a panic. Aristaeus, with a nasty grin on his face chased after her this way and that she blindly ran getting further and further away from the safety of her husband and the wedding guests. Then, tragedy, not looking where she was going she trod on a poisonous snake which bit her ankle and she fell down dying. Orpheus who had been searching for his wife saw her in the distance laying on the ground. He rushed to her and gently lifted her head, tears filled his eyes as he could see the pain she was in, their eyes met and tenderly he kissed her on the lips.

As they kissed Eurydice quietly passed away, the last kiss lingering on her lips, that last brief moment of happiness. The god Hermes appeared and with the utmost delicacy took her hand and led her to the Underworld.

Poor Orpheus was distraught, his eyes blind with tears, how cruel life was to him to lose his beloved on their wedding day. He vowed in front of the assembled guests that he would never love another or play and sing again. The ladies were upset at this, they had all been secretly in love with him, hoping he might take one of them for his wife. Orpheus sat under the oak tree where he had first met Eurydice, trying to control his thoughts. Slowly his mind cleared when he had a sudden idea. If his music had such magical effects why not use those powers in an attempt to obtain Eurydice's release from the Underworld by charming its king and queen, Hades and Persephone into granting her freedom. It really was a dangerous and desperate plan as no one had ever before been returned from death to life. He was prepared to try even though he knew if his plan failed he would lose his own life.

Orpheus set sail across the Ionian sea searching for the entrance to the Underworld. All the time he played his music charming the winds to carry him to his destination. Eventually he landed on the coast of Thesprotia where the river Acheron disappears underground. This was a gloomy place where the sun never shone, but here hidden by tall poplars and willows was the entrance to the Underworld. According to Homer in his Odyssey these poplars quickly shed their seeds. Orpheus carefully picked his way through them and followed the banks of the river underground into the gloomy depths beyond.

It was very eerie and frightening especially as he heard moaning, groaning and growling sounds all around him which got louder the deeper he went on the downward path and sometimes there were also ear piercing screams. He was very scared and was shaking too much to play his lyre which he nearly dropped when suddenly he felt some slimy creatures drop on him and slither silently away. He shuddered and almost gave up, but his deep love for Eurydice gave him courage and the thought of seeing her again spurred him on.

Eventually he came to the subterranean river Styx, which had to be crossed to reach the Kingdom of Hades. The dog Cerberus was on guard here. He was not an ordinary dog, he had three heads, serpents bristled on his back and from his mouth dribbled black venom. He would let no one pass unless they fed him with a honey cake, but never again would he let them come out. With trembling hands Orpheus commenced playing his lyre which so charmed the dog that he made no attempt to stop Orpheus passing on.

Orpheus came to the bank of the river Styx where Charon, the ferryman, stood waiting to take the dead across the river. This was the only way to reach the other side and Charon firmly refused to perform this task unless he was paid, that is why a coin was always placed in the mouth of people when they died so that they could pay him, otherwise they would never reach the other side and would have to stay forever wandering about on the gloomy deserted shore. Orpheus again used the magical charm of his music to persuade the grumbling and difficult ferryman to take him across the dark river Styx.

Once on the other side Orpheus gained more confidence and walked on until he finally came to the great hall where King Hades sat on his throne next to his queen Persephone. They were interviewing the newly arrived before sending them to be judged and sentenced by the three judges of the dead, Minos, Rhadamanthys and Aeacus. If they had led a good life they were sent to Elysium. This was the abode of heroes and the righteous, a place of perfect happiness. If, however, they had been wicked and so unwise as to offend the gods, they were sent to Tartarus, a place of punishment. Of course those sent to Tartarus wished they had led a better life, but by now it was too late. Hades was both surprised and annoyed that a live mortal had penetrated his underworld kingdom and demanded to know what the intruder was doing there when he had not been sent for. Orpheus boldly exclaimed that he had come for Eurydice, to take her back with him. Hades glared at him in astonishment and growled in an ugly voice that this was quite impossible; he angrily continued that for his insolence Orpheus would be held and confined to Tartarus. Hades wife, Persephone, could not help feeling sorry for the musician when she could see how great his love was for Eurydice, and when Orpheus started to play and sing her heart melted and she longed for the time when she would return to earth, which she did each year at summer time when all vegetation started to grow and the flowers blossomed. The more she listened, the more enchanted she became, even the dark frown on Hades face softened. He glared at his wife whom he loved dearly and seeing the tears in her eyes wondered that if he was in the same situation as Orpheus whether he would have enough courage to risk all for her as this young man was doing for his beloved. Love must be stronger than death, and with these thoughts in mind and captivated by the wonderful music in his ears, he felt that he must reward Orpheus for his most pleasing musical performance.

In his most official voice, Hades announced to all concerned that it was his royal command that Orpheus may return to earth with Eurydice. He must return the way he came and Eurydice would follow him, but, and here was his final ruling, Orpheus must, under no circumstances look back at her until he had reached the upper world. Orpheus was overwhelmed with happiness and he departed, playing and singing, his heart full of joy. How he longed to reach the upper world and hold his beloved Eurydice in his arms again. On and on he went the journey seeming much longer than before and never ending, he was growing impatient, but, at last, he crossed the river Styx and stopped playing. He now only had to ascend the dark passageway to daylight and freedom.

Ahead of him he could see the light of day and could hear the birds singing, he was almost there, back in the land of the living. Suddenly he realised that he could not hear Eurydice's footsteps behind him, but of course the dead make no sound. He stopped and listened for her breathing, he could hear nothing, not a sound. He called her name, she did not answer. He pleaded with her not to ignore him, was she really behind him? His mind was in a turmoil, he gave a silent prayer to the gods that she was really following him. She was, but his mind was now so full of doubts he could bear the suspense no longer. He was just about to step out into the daylight when he turned his head very slightly attempting to get just a glimpse of her to regain his confidence. He caught sight of her, but as he did she faded away before his eyes. She had gone back to the underworld never to return.

It is easy to imagine how sad and distraught Orpheus was, he was inconsolable. All the ladies of Thrace, where he lived, wished him to choose another wife.

In fact, they all wanted him for themselves and started to quarrel over him He would have nothing to do with them and spurned them. This attitude made then very annoyed and angry, so much so that once when they had been to the ceremony of the god of wine, Dionysus, they had drunk so much in the god's honour that they became inebriated. In their maddened drunken state they searched for Orpheus, caught him and killed him. They cut off his head and threw it into the river Hebrus where it floated away to Lesbos.

Orpheus' head was washed ashore on Lesbos and the local people buried it with all reverence and respect and built a shrine to him. It was for this kind deed that the people of Lesbos were rewarded with the gift of poetic skill and, even to this day, the nightingales in the olive trees sing more sweetly there than anywhere else in the world.

HERACLES

Zeus who could see from his throne on Olympus many things that were happening on earth realised that all was not well: not only were there monsters causing havoc and great distress among the people in many parts of the land, but some of the people themselves were behaving badly: they did not worship the gods or sacrifice to them; they bullied and made war on their peace loving neighbours. If things carried on the way they were, only thieves and murderers would be left! It was a terrible thought and he must do something to save the Greek nation not only from these bad men but also from the terrible monsters.

Wise Zeus decided that the only way to salvation was for a hero to set an example: a man strong and powerful enough to stand up to and overpower these brutal men and monsters! This hero must be born of a mortal woman and be capable of suffering and of resisting temptation. It would be of no use to send an immortal god, because people would know he was different from them, especially as he could not suffer pain or hunger or even be put to death. It must be one of their own kind in order to gain their confidence and support to free mankind from many evils. As Zeus loved the Greeks he decided that it should be his son who would be their saviour. He looked on earth for a good woman, honest, pure and devout and he chose a lady by the name of Alcmene. She was betrothed to King Amphitryon, (who was away on an expedition in another part of the country) and she had promised to marry him on his return, after he had captured and punished a band of robbers who had killed her brothers. In his search for them he came to Thebes where Creon, the king, promised to help capture the robbers if Amphitryon would rid his country of the Teumiessian Vixen. This vicious animal, which everyday killed and ate children, belonged to the god Dionysus. It was enchanted, making it impossible for it ever to be caught. How then could it be got rid of? The task seemed impossible!

Amphitryon, however, had an idea; he prayed to Artemis the goddess of hunting and asked if he might borrow her dog which was called Laelaps, and was destined to always capture whatever prey it chased. Artemis heard his prayer and allowed him to borrow Laelaps. When Zeus saw what was happening he was very worried, on the one hand there was a magic dog which would always catch its prey and, on the other hand, a magic vixen which would always escape! The problem seemed unanswerable. He solved it by turning them both into stone. Amphitryon, with Creon's help, was now able to capture and punish the robbers; he then sent word to Alcmene that he was on his way home and asked her to make arrangements for the wedding on his arrival.

Alcmene was delighted and when she saw the person she thought was Amphitryon arrive earlier than expected. She was overjoyed and they married straight away. Of course, she had no idea it was Zeus who had changed himself to look like Amphitryon! Zeus made the wedding night last the length of three days by ordering Helios, the sun god, not to drive his chariot across the sky. He commanded Silene, the moon goddess, to go slowly, and Hypnos, the god of sleep to make mankind so drowsy no one would realise what was happening.

When Amphitryon eventually arrived, you can imagine how surprised he was to hear that he was apparently already married! (A messenger was sent by the gods to explain the situation to him and, that now Alcmene was his wife, he must never tell her that Zeus was really her first husband.) When Alcmene was nearing the time when she would give birth to a child, Zeus knew that this was to be the son he wanted who was destined to save mankind. He was so pleased he called all the gods together and told them that the next child Eileithyia, the goddess of childbirth, brought forth, would rule over his neighbours. Of course he was expecting this to be his child by Alcmene.

He then went on to tell them that the child would be called Heracles, which means the 'glory of Hera'. She, (that is Hera), was the wife of Zeus and she was very angry because she knew nothing of her husband's plan to have a son by a mortal woman. Zeus could see she was annoyed and when she asked him to swear the unbreakable oath of the River Styx, (the river of Hades), that he would not change his mind, he quickly agreed. Carefully making sure no one was looking she visited

Alcmene and by using witchcraft delayed the birth of Heracles until Eileithyia induced Nicippe, Queen of Tiryns, who was also pregnant to have her child first. This was a boy named Eurystheus and he was now destined to become ruler over Heracles.

You can imagine how furious Zeus was to have his plans thwarted but, of course, he could not go back on his oath. However, he did manage to get Hera to agree that when the boys reached manhood, if Heracles performed ten Labours set for him by Eurystheus his son would become a god. And so it was that Heracles was born after Eurystheus, but at the same time Alcmene gave birth to another boy named Iphicles who, although he was the twin of Heracles, was the son of Amphitryon and not Zeus. Amphitryon knew that only one of the boys was his son but he had no idea which one it was, so he decided he must find out.

The boys were ten months old when he put them to the test. They had been put to bed for the night on a large bronze shield with lambs' fleece for blankets. At midnight Amphitryon peeped into their room and seeing them sleeping peacefully, quickly dropped two snakes on the floor of their nursery. The snakes slithered across the floor making their way to the two sleeping boys. They both awoke and Iphicles, seeing the snakes in front of him, screamed with fright and tried to run away. Heracles simply smiled and grasping a snake in each hand with his tiny but strong fingers squeezed the wriggling reptiles, shaking and shaking them until they were dead!!

Amphitryon looked at Iphicles crouching on the floor, his eyes full of terror and then he looked at Heracles who was smiling and gurgling with delight. Now he knew that Heracles was the son of Zeus and Iphicles was his son.

As a boy Heracles was taught to read and write and to sing and play the lyre. As he grew older he learnt to how to fight with sword and spear, to use a bow and arrow, and to box and wrestle. He was a quick learner and excelled in all these activities, but unfortunately he had a violent temper which he could not always control. When he was still only a boy learning to play the lyre his teacher, Linus, boxed his ears for playing a wrong note. Heracles temper got the better of him and he flared up striking Linus a terrific blow with the lyre which, sad to say, killed him. Heracles was charged with murder but pleaded, successfully, by quoting an ancient Greek law that force was justifiable when used to resist aggression. Amphitryon, fearing that more trouble might be caused by the boy's violent temper sent him away to grow up out of harm's way on a farm in the country looking after the cattle.

One day, when he was sitting in a field watching the cattle, he heard a lady's voice calling his name. Looking up he was surprised to see two ladies approaching him. One was wearing colourful clothes , many fine jewels and too much make-up. She told Heracles that one of her names was 'Pleasure' and the others were 'Vice' and 'Folly' and that, as he was now of an age to choose his path in life, he should follow her: then he would have an easy and enjoyable life not having to worry about other people's problems. Just then the other lady reached Heracles, she wore a plain white dress and her kind face expressed goodness, truth and wisdom. She told him her name was 'Virtue' and that to follow her path would not be easy, but, if he did, he would do great and noble deeds and help many people. His life would be hard, but through his struggles and sufferings not only would he have a clear conscience but he would be rewarded in heaven.

Heracles chose to follow the path of Virtue, and the ladies then disappeared from view. Shortly after this experience he was to perform his first act of heroism. For several months a savage lion had been causing farmers great distress. Heracles made a promise he would slay this lion before it could do more damage. He made himself a large club from an olive tree and set off in search of the lion. He tracked it to its lair and boldly attacked the lion. Although it was strong it was no match for Heracles, who kept smiting its head with his club. The lion collapsed on the ground, its head spinning, and Heracles was able to kill it with a swift thrust of his knife. Later, he came across another lion that was not so easy to overcome. News of Heracles strength and bravery spread throughout Greece. King Creon of Thebes sent word to him asking for his help to save his country. A neighbouring King by the name of Eriginus held Thebes under his tribute and was making unreasonable and excessive demands. Thebes would soon be reduced to starvation. As Heracles had chosen the path of helping others, he came to the rescue of Creon. When Eriginus heard the news he was livid with rage and set out to completely destroy Thebes. Heracles, however, ambushed his army in a narrow mountain pass and completely annihilated them single handed. Creon was overcome with joy and relief and rewarded Heracles by giving him Megara, his beautiful daughter's hand in marriage. Heracles was delighted to have such a beautiful wife and for several years they lived blissfully together and had three sons whom Heracles adored. This state of happiness unfortunately did not last, Hera, who did not like Heracles took control of his mind and sent him mad. One day when Heracles sat watching his children at play he suddenly saw the sun go black and felt a terrible pain in his head, he staggered to his feet, his mind confused, and, where his children were he thought he saw enemies attacking; grasping his sword he rushed to kill them not realising that he was slaying his own children! When he recovered from his madness he was overcome with grief and asked the oracle what he must do to be forgiven for this terrible deed that he had committed. He was told that he must present himself to King Eurystheus and obey his commands. Heracles hated this idea because Eurystheus was a weak coward and, like all cowards, treated his subjects as though they were dirt beneath his feet. Heracles was in deep despair. He was loathe to serve such an inferior, repulsive individual, but he knew he must be a dutiful son and obey the wishes of

Zeus. Of course, Eurystheus was overjoyed that he had been given the power to order Heracles to do his bidding. He set him twelve of the hardest tasks he could think of certain that he would not be able to survive them. These became known as the 'Twelve Labours of Heracles' (Hercules). Originally there were ten, but as you will see Eurystheus would not count two of them so Heracles was obliged to accomplish two more, making twelve in all.

THE TWELVE LABOURS OF HERACLES

The Nemean Lion

The first labour Eurystheus ordered Heracles to perform, was to bring him the skin of the Nemean Lion from the valley of Nemea which lay a few miles from Mycene. (The ruins of Mycene can still be seen and amongst these is the famous Lion's gate built with huge stones. The stones of the arch above where the great door used to be, were carved with two lions which can be seen to this day.)

Heracles took a long time searching for the lion as there was no one to ask where it was, as they had either been devoured by the lion or were afraid to leave their homes! Eventually he managed to track it to its lair in the rocks which were covered with bones and blood of men and cattle. Taking careful aim with his bow he let fly an arrow straight at the lion's head; it was a perfect shot but the arrow simply bounced off the animal. Heracles picked up his sword and smote a mighty blow on the back of its neck, but the sword just bent! This lion could not be harmed by any weapon even if it were made of stone or metal, in fact the lion who had been sleeping had hardly noticed what Heracles had been doing. Suddenly, it opened an eye, gave a great yawn, then spotted Heracles and licked its lips thinking here was another tasty meal, and without warning sprang at Heracles. He side-stepped the animal and at the same time struck its head a terrific blow with his club just as once before he had done to the another lion. This time though, the club just broke into splinters. The lion shook its head, not because it had been hurt but because the blow had caused a ringing in its ears. Thus, the lion was off-guard and Heracles sprang onto its back and putting both arms around its neck he squeezed as hard as he could. The lion twisted and turned and even rolled over on its back, but Heracles refused to let go; he even tightened his grip on the lion's throat. The lion grew weaker and weaker until there was no movement and Heracles realised that it was finally dead; throttled by his powerful arms!

The next problem was how to skin the animal as no knife or weapon was sharp enough or strong enough to make the slightest impression on its carcass, but skin it he did by using the lion's own claws. He wrapped the skin over his shoulders and wore it like a cloak with its front paws over his shoulders to keep it in place. He wore its head, (even though it was still attached to the skin), like a hat!

When Heracles confronted Eurystheus wearing the skin of the Nemean lion, Eurystheus nearly jumped out of his own skin and shaking with fear he ordered Heracles to go on his second labour which was to destroy the Lernaean Hydra.

The Lernaean Hydra

The Hydra was a large water serpent with nine heads, not only was its bite poisonous but its foul breath was also deadly. It lived in the marshy swamps of Lerna not far from Argos.

Heracles set out in his chariot which was driven by Iolaus, his nephew and great friend. Arriving at the edge of the swamp, they saw the serpent in the distance and Heracles shot at it with burning arrows. Although the arrows hit their target they did not harm the Hydra but only drew its attention to Heracles so that it raised its ugly heads and attacked fiercely. Holding his breath to protect himself from the poisonous fumes, Heracles swung his club and shattered its nearest head. To his horror two heads immediately grew in its place. He swung his club with renewed vigour, but every time he knocked off a head, two more would suddenly grow. To add to his troubles, a giant crab came scuttling out of the marsh to help the Hydra and bit Heracles' foot! With a cry of pain and anger Heracles crushed it with his other foot. (The image of the crab can be seen in the sky at night, as it became a constellation and one of the twelve signs of the Zodiac). That was one danger out of the way, but there was still the problem of the Hydra's heads.

He called to Iolaus to fetch a branch of burning wood and each time he knocked off a head he thrust the flame into the shattered neck, this seared the neck sealing it so that new heads would not grow from its bleeding stumps.

Finally there was just one head left, but this one was immortal: it could not die. Heracles cut this head completely off and buried it, still hissing, under a huge stone, (it is probably there to this day, certainly the swamp is a breeding ground for poisonous snakes). Heracles then dipped the tips of his arrows into the bile of the reptile's carcass which made them so poisonous that even the slightest scratch from them would be fatal.

Eurystheus was so annoyed that Heracles had returned safely he refused to count this labour because of the help given by Iolaus!

The Ceryneian Hind

The third labour given to Heracles was to capture and bring back alive the Ceryneian Hind. This creature had golden horns and belonged to the goddess Artemis. Originally there were five of these hinds and Artemis had captured four to pull her chariot. The fifth she allowed to wander free over the hills of Arcadia, but no one would dare touch this beautiful animal because it was sacred to Artemis. Heracles dare not hurt it and chased the hind for a whole year before he finally managed to capture the animal as it lay exhausted under a tree. Gently he lifted it onto his shoulders and started his return journey. On his way he met Artemis, who said how very upset and annoyed she was that he had treated one of her favourite animals with such disrespect. moreover she saw no reason why she should not slay him where he stood with one of her golden arrows. Heracles replied that he would be quite happy to depart from this world, Zeus had ordered him to obey the commands of Eurystheus, a weak and bombastic coward, and it was so humiliating for him. Artemis felt sorry for Heracles and said he may take the hind to Eurystheus, although he must return it unharmed or she would punish both him and Eurystheus. Heracles delivered her message to Eurystheus who became terrified in case anything happened to the hind, he wished he had not set this labour and pleaded with Heracles to return it safely. Of course, as soon as Heracles had done so his attitude changed, and he again became the boastful and contemptuous bully and sent Heracles on his fourth labour. This was to capture and bring back alive a fierce wild boar that lived on Mount Erymanthus.

The Erymanthian Boar

So savage was this beast that no man would go near it. In the course of his journey Heracles had to pass through the land of the Centaurs. These creatures had a man's head, shoulders, arms and body to their waist and below this they had the body and legs of a horse. They were half man and half horse. Pholus, one of these Centaurs, invited Heracles to dinner and opened a jar of wine for him as a special treat. It was delicious wine and very old. Soon the other Centaurs could smell its beautiful aroma and came crowding around. They snatched the jar of wine and passed it to one another , each one greedily drinking great draughts. As they were not used to drinking wine they soon began to feel strange and the more they drank of this strong drink the stranger they felt, they all thought they had been poisoned and attacked Heracles. Pholus was frightened and galloped away to hide leaving Heracles to face the angry Centaurs alone. Heracles fought them off with his poisoned arrows, killing some while the rest ran away. Now the fight was over Pholus returned and was amazed to see that a mere arrow had so easily killed these powerful creatures, he picked up one to examine it. Unfortunately he dropped it and it grazed his foot; the poison of the Hydra was still on the tip of the arrow and, indeed, was so strong that Pholus died within minutes.

Heracles continued his search for the Boar until at last he found it in its lair. Skilfully he drove it uphill into the snow clad mountain, until the beast lay down exhausted. Heracles then tied its legs together, heaved it onto his powerful shoulders and carried it back to Eurystheus who was so scared when he saw the boar he hid himself in a large jar, gibbering with fear. Heracles laughed, untied the boar's legs and threw it into the sea where it swam away to safety.

For his fifth labour, Heracles was ordered to clean the stables of King Augeias in a single day.

The Stables of Augeias

Augeias had the largest stables in the whole of Greece and they had not been cleaned for three years, so you can imagine what a mess they must have been in. The smell was awful and the filth had even spread to the pastures in the valley which could no longer be ploughed. Heracles surprised Augeias by offering to clean out his stables in one day, and finish it before nightfall if he would give him a tenth of his cattle. Believing this task to be impossible, Augeias agreed willingly.

First Heracles knocked holes in the walls at either end of the stables and then dug a trench from them to a nearby river. The diverted water poured down the channels he had made and through the gaps in the walls and the strong current swept away all the dirt, not only cleaning the stables but also the pastures in the valley. After this he filled in the trenches and repaired the holes he had made in the walls. The stables were now as clean as a new pin, but Augeias would not keep his part of the bargain and refused to part with any of his cattle, claiming that Heracles had only been carrying out the orders of Eurystheus. To make matters worse Eurystheus would not count this labour as one of the ten, because Heracles had worked for hire.

Heracles sixth labour was to remove the Stymphalian birds.

The Stymphalian Birds

These birds as large a herons had brazen claws, feathers, beaks and wings and were able to shoot their feathers with deadly accuracy at passers-by and having killed them would eat their bodies! Sometimes they attacked in a flock, swooping down and flying straight at men piercing them with their beaks that were so sharp they could even pierce armour. These birds lived in a marsh at Stymphalus and Heracles found he could not get near them because the ground was so soft he would sink. Athene came to his aid and lent him a pair of bronze castanets as big as dustbin lids, which he took with him to a mountain overlooking the Stymphalian marsh. He then clashed them together and the loud din they made startled the birds so much that they flew into the air. Heracles managed to shoot a lot of them down and the rest flew away.

His seventh labour was to catch the Cretan Bull.

The Cretan Bull

Heracles sailed to the beautiful island of Crete where Minos, the King of this country, made him welcome. Minos was delighted that Heracles had come to capture this bull because it had gone mad and was trampling crops all over the countryside and nobody could do a thing about it. However, Heracles was so strong that he was able to overpower the bull and carry it back to Eurystheus.

Seeing the bull before him Eurystheus went white with fear and again jumped into a large jar to hide. He trembled with fright and would not come out until Heracles had sent the bull away. When it was safe he emerged from the jar and sent Heracles on his eighth labour which was to capture the mares of Diomedes.

The Mares of Diomedes

There were four of these animals and they were kept chained in their stables by the cruel Diomedes who fed them on human flesh. These horses were very vicious and would attack and eat anyone who came too near them. Heracles, however, managed to tame them. He did this by first attacking Diomedes with his club and then feeding him to his own horses. After eating him the mares immediately became tame and docile.

Heracles was able to take them to Eurystheus without any trouble. Eurystheus now sent Heracles to fetch the girdle of Hippolyte, the Queen of the Amazons as his ninth labour.

The Girdle of Hippolyte

Amazons were a warrior tribe of women who fought like men, and the god Ares had given Hippolyte, their leader, a magnificent golden girdle. Now Eurystheus had a daughter named Admete and she told her father that she would dearly love to have that girdle more than anything else in the world and so Heracles was sent to fetch it for her.

When Hippolyte met Heracles she was so impressed by this strong handsome young man that she fell in love with him. Willingly she offered to give him the girdle if only he would take her away with him to which he readily agreed. The other Amazons seeing them leave together thought that their queen was being taken prisoner and they rushed to rescue her. Luckily Heracles had brought some friends with him and they were able to beat off the Amazons. But unfortunately Heracles, thinking that Hippolyte had betrayed him, killed her and took the girdle!

Heracles tenth labour was to fetch some cattle that belonged to Geryon.

The Cattle of Geryon

Geryon was the strongest man in the world and from his waist grew three bodies with six arms and three heads. His cattle were guarded by Orthrus, a vicious two headed dog, and by the herdsman, Eurytion.

Heracles had a long journey in front to him, he had to pass through the Straits of Gibraltar to reach his destination. In those days people thought that there was nothing but sea after these straits, and Heracles erected two pillars on either side to mark the limit of how far it was possible for people to travel. These became known as the Pillars of Heracles (or Hercules).

When Eurytion saw Heracles approaching in the distance he sent Orthrus, the dog, to attack him. This two headed dog, snarling and baring its teeth, attacked Heracles, who swiftly jumped aside and at the same time brought his club down on one of the dog's heads. This head was now lifeless and in a flash Heracles smote the other head killing the animal instantly. Seeing the dog was dead, Eurytion, the herdsman, attacked but received the same treatment.

With a roar of rage Geryon who, with his three bodies was the strongest man in the world, rushed at Heracles. Heracles knew his strength was not equal to Geryon's so he ran quickly round to the side of him from where he was able to fire a poisoned arrow that went right through all three of Geryon's bodies, thus killing him.

Driving the cattle back he won many hearts by helping people. Heracles had now completed ten labours, but as Eurystheus refused to count the second and the fifth he had two more to do. His eleventh was to fetch the golden apples that were guarded by the daughters of Atlas, who were known as the Hesperides.

The Apples of the Hesperides

The Hesperides were helped in the task of guarding the apples by a dragon called Ladon who coiled himself around the tree.

Heracles had no idea in which direction the garden of the Hesperides lay, so he decided to ask directions from their father Atlas who, of course, was holding up the heavens. Atlas told him that it was a secret where this garden was situated, but added that he would willingly collect the golden apples for him if he would hold up the heavens while he was away. Heracles agreed although he had not realised how heavy the heavens were, and as he struggled to steady himself some of the stars were shaken off, but at last he managed to stand firm.

He was certainly very relieved when Atlas returned with the apples and could hardly wait to give him back the heavens. However, Atlas, now that he had tasted freedom, was not at all keen to have this burden back. He told Heracles he would do him a great favour by taking the golden apples to Eurystheus himself; then return immediately to take back the task of holding up the heavens.

Heracles realised at once that he had been tricked and that Atlas would not return, so he pretended to be pleased with the suggestion and told Atlas that he should have a much needed holiday but, as he was not used to carrying such a heavy weight, he asked Atlas if he would please hold the heavens for just a few minutes while he put a pad on his head. Atlas put the golden apples on the ground and took the heavens from Heracles who, smiling to himself, quickly picked up the apples and, shouting farewell to the dismayed Atlas, hurried back to Eurystheus.

On his way he passed through Libya, whose cruel king Antaeus forced all strangers to wrestle with him. He always won and killed his opponents, using their skulls to decorate a temple. Antaeus had an unfair advantage over other men because as he was the son of Ge (Mother Earth), she renewed his power each time he touched her.

Heracles was determined to stop Antaeus from killing other innocent strangers. He rubbed oil all over his body making it slippery and difficult to grip. The fight started and Heracles had Antaeus in a powerful hold, squeezing so hard that the breath went out of his body, he then flung Antaeus to the ground. To his amazement Antaeus recovered his strength and viciously attacked him with renewed vigour. Again Heracles getting the better of his opponent threw him with great force onto the floor. As soon as Antaeus touched the earth his muscles became larger and more powerful and, with loud roar, he attacked again. Heracles was rapidly getting weaker after using all his strength and energy throwing Antaeus, and he realised that every time Antaeus touched the ground he grew even stronger.

With his remaining strength Heracles lifted Antaeus in the air not letting any part of his body touch the earth. Antaeus struggled and struggled trying to get free and throw himself onto the ground so that Mother Earth would give him more strength, but the longer he was off the earth the weaker he became until Heracles managed to squeeze the last drop of breath out of his body, thus ridding the country of this terrible man.

We now come to the twelfth and final labour.

The Capture of Cerberus

Eurystheus was in despair of ever getting rid of Heracles so he made the last labour the most difficult one by ordering him to fetch the dog Cerberus. This, he thought was impossible because Cerberus was the hound that guarded the gates of the Underworld. As I have already told you in the tale of Orpheus and the Underworld he was a truly frightful dog, with three heads and tail that was barbed with many sharp pointed spikes like fish hooks.

The god Hermes helped Heracles find his way to the river Styx, this was the underground river which had to be crossed to reach the Kingdom of Hades, who ruled over the dead. Waiting with a boat was Charon the ferryman who was an ugly smelly old man who wore a permanent scowl. He was only supposed to take dead souls across the stream and always demanded money first (already mentioned on page 88, in the tale of Orpheus and Eurydice). He refused to take living persons across until Heracles, scowling fiercely, frightened him so much that he dare not refuse.

Once on the other side, Heracles found himself in the land of the dead and saw many who had been wicked and were being punished. There was Ixion who once tried to lure Hera away from Zeus, he was tied to a wheel of fire which never stopped rolling.

He saw Tantalus who, because he had tried to deceive the gods, was condemned to stand in a stream of clear water which each time he bent forward to drink and quench his burning thirst would recede leaving only mud. Above his head hung beautiful, succulent fruit, but as soon as he reached for some the wind would gently blow the fruit just that little bit too far away for him to pluck.

There was also Sisyphus, a robber and murderer who just before he died instructed his wife not to bury him. When he did die and went to the Underworld he told Persephone, the wife of Hades, that he should not have been allowed across the River Styx because he was unburied. Therefore, if she would allow him to return to the upper world he would arrange for his own burial and return within three days. Persephone granted his request, but Sisyphus broke his promise and stayed on earth. In the end Hermes forced him back and he was punished by having to roll a huge stone up a hill to the other side. He struggled with this stone, his muscles aching, and each time he reached the brow of the hill that stone would roll back down to the bottom and he would have to start all over again.

Heracles was not the first man to find his way to the Underworld, some years before two friends of his, Theseus and Peiritheous, had found their way there. They had done this out of curiosity and a sense of adventure, which of course you have read about in the chapter Theseus visits the Underworld.

When at last Heracles met Hades and Persephone he asked permission to borrow Cerberus. Hades willingly agreed provided that he could master the dog without using weapons.

Heracles gripped the animal by the throat from which rose the three heads. Snarling and snapping it viciously lashed its barbed tail, but Heracles was protected by the tough lion's skin that he always wore. In the end Heracles strength was too much for Cerberus and he was forced to submit and be dragged from the Underworld into the sun. Not being used to daylight, the sun hurt the dog's eyes, he struggled and barked and saliva dribbled from his mouth which, as soon as it touched the ground, grew into a poisonous flower called Aconite.

When Heracles took Cerberus to Eurystheus he screamed in terror and trembling with fear, once again, hid himself in a large jar. He pleaded with Heracles that now he had completed his twelve labours to take the dog away and never come back. Heracles returned Cerberus to his home in the Underworld delighted that he was no longer at the beck and call of Eurystheus.

FURTHER ADVENTURES OF HERACLES

Now that he was free from servitude, Heracles did not rest on his laurels, but carried on with his chosen life fighting bad men and dangerous monsters.

One day after many adventures a young man named Iphitus asked Heracles to help him search for his stolen cattle.

Iphitus actually suspected Heracles of stealing them and thought that, by asking him for his help, he would catch him out. When Heracles realised what Iphitus was thinking he was so furious that his temper got the better of him and in his anger he killed Iphitus. Immediately, he was sorry but, of course, it was too late.

He went to Delphi to ask the Oracle what he must do to be forgiven. The priestess, who interpreted the oracles, refused to give him an answer. Heracles' quick temper flared up again and angrily he picked up the tripod (the seat on which the priestess sat) and began to carry it off. Storming out of the Temple, he bumped into the god Apollo, who just happened to be paying a visit to his temple. Apollo, furiously, grabbed one leg of the tripod demanding its release. Heracles, still full of anger, refused and a tug-of-war started between them. Who would have won? We do not know, because Zeus stopped the argument telling them how silly they both were, and that they would only break the tripod. He also said "they must make friends, and Apollo must give Heracles his answer".

So they shook hands and Apollo told Heracles that he must be sold as a slave and the money paid for him given to the parents of Iphitus, the man he had killed.

It was Omphale, Queen of Lydia, who bought Heracles. Although, he was sold as a nameless slave, Omphale paid the high price of three silver Talents for him, though this was actually a bargain! Heracles worked well for Omphale, ridding her country of many robbers and vagabonds.

It so happened that near Ephesus lived twin brothers, known as the Cercopes, who were expert cheats and liars. They were always full of mischief, just like monkeys, in fact, they even looked like monkeys.

Heracles caught them trying to steal from him as he lay asleep and decided to teach them a lesson. He tied their feet to a long pole, which he put across his shoulders, and carried them away upside down. Being upside down they, naturally, saw their surroundings from an unusual position which they thought very funny; especially the way the lion's skin Heracles was wearing kept bouncing up an down, like a kilt swaying in the wind. This made them laugh loudly. Heracles was puzzled, but when they told him what was so funny, he had to chuckle himself. The Cercopes amused Heracles so much that, finally, he let them go with a caution.

Of course he had other adventures, which were more serious and dangerous!

One concerned a man named Syleus, who would force passers-by to work all day in his vineyard without rest or food. When they fell down exhausted, he would cut their throats. Heracles tore up all his vines by the roots and then killed Syleus.

Another cruel man was Lityerses, who forced strangers to reap his harvest and, as soon as they slowed down, he would whip them unmercifully. Heracles, being much stronger, picked him up bodily and threw him into a river.

Roaming the countryside was a gigantic serpent that killed and ate people and destroyed all the crops. Heracles shot it dead with his poisoned arrows.

You can imaging how pleased Omphale was with him, so much so, that when she went on holiday in the country she took Heracles with her as a treat.

In the countryside lived the god Pan, a mischievous god who loved to play tricks on people. One of his favourite tricks was: to creep up silently on a sleeping shepherd and give a loud, terrifying, high pitched shriek in his ear. Of course, the poor shepherd would wake up startled and from this trick of Pan's we get the word 'panic'.

Seeing Omphale in all her rich robes and finery, Pan fell in love with her and decided to ask her to marry him.

That evening, after Omphale and Heracles had had their supper, they sat talking. Omphale admired the lion's skin Heracles was wearing and suggested, just for fun, that they swop clothes. She thought it would be amusing to see the manly Heracles in lady's clothes, while she wore his. They exchanged clothes and had a good laugh; then retired for the night to their separate rooms.

Pan, having decided that now was the time to ask Omphale to marry him, went to their quarters in the dark, and seeing Heracles still wearing Omphales' clothes thought it was her. He crept up and whispered words of love in his ear, asking for his hand in marriage. You can imagine Heracles' surprise. He kicked Pan across the room where the poor fellow landed with a mighty thud, knocking all the breath out of his body. Omphale, hearing all the commotion, called for lights and seeing poor old Pan sprawled on the floor, looking so bewildered, both she and Heracles laughed and laughed.

The tables finally had been turned on Pan for all the tricks that he had played on others.

Omphale admired Heracles so much and was so pleased with all the help he had given her that she now restored his freedom.

Heracles bade her farewell and travelled to the other end of Greece where he met and fell in love with a beautiful lady named Deinareira.

It so happened that the river god Achelous wanted Deinareira for his wife and challenged Heracles to a wrestling match, the winner to marry her.

Achelous had a nasty habit of changing himself into different shapes; sometimes into a bull, sometimes into a speckled serpent and at other times into a man with a bull's head.

All this was very confusing and worrying to Deinareira and she was not at all happy about it, and so was delighted when a real man sought her hand in marriage.

She watched anxiously as the two rivals fought. Heracles threw Achelous on the ground, but he changed his shape into a serpent who wriggled out of reach, then changing into the shape of a bull, and, breathing fire from his nostrils, he charged head down, sharp horns pointed directly at Heracles. Heracles was too quick for him and side stepped at the last minute, and grasping hold of his horns, flung him on the ground with such force that one of the horns broke off. Achelous gave in and Heracles married Deinareira.